FINANCING PRESIDENTIAL CAMPAIGNS

Delmer D. Dunn

FINANCING PRESIDENTIAL CAMPAIGNS

Studies in Presidential Selection
THE BROOKINGS INSTITUTION
Washington, D.C.

Copyright © 1972 by
THE BROOKINGS INSTITUTION
1775 Massachusetts Avenue, N.W., Washington, D.C. 20036

Library of Congress Cataloging in Publication Data:

Dunn, Delmer D
 Financing presidential campaigns.
 (Studies in presidential selection)
 Includes bibliographical references.
 1. Elections—U.S.—Campaign funds.
 2. Presidents—U.S.—Election.   I. Title.
 II. Series.
JK1991.D85   329'.025'0973   72-000064
ISBN 0-8157-1962-0
ISBN 0-8157-1961-2 (pbk.)

1 2 3 4 5 6 7 8 9

THE BROOKINGS INSTITUTION is an independent organization devoted to nonpartisan research, education, and publication in economics, government, foreign policy, and the social sciences generally. Its principal purposes are to aid in the development of sound public policies and to promote public understanding of issues of national importance.

The Institution was founded on December 8, 1927, to merge the activities of the Institute for Government Research, founded in 1916, the Institute of Economics, founded in 1922, and the Robert Brookings Graduate School of Economics and Government, founded in 1924.

The general administration of the Institution is the responsibility of a Board of Trustees charged with maintaining the independence of the staff and fostering the most favorable conditions for creative research and education. The immediate direction of the policies, program, and staff of the Institution is vested in the President, assisted by an advisory committee of the officers and staff.

In publishing a study, the Institution presents it as a competent treatment of a subject worthy of public consideration. The interpretations and conclusions in such publications are those of the author or authors and do not necessarily reflect the views of the other staff members, officers, or trustees of the Brookings Institution.

FOREWORD

THIS BOOK deals with a critical problem of American democracy: the rising costs of campaigning for national public office. Current reform efforts range from imposing an absolute limit on expenditures to providing public money directly to candidates. All share an assumption that costs are too high. Much of the recent expansion in total costs can be attributed to rapidly increased spending for broadcast time, and reform plans center on devices to finance or to control such expenditures. Mr. Dunn's study consequently emphasizes broadcast-oriented plans. In investigating costs, legislative proposals advanced to control them, reactions to such proposals, and their likely impact, Mr. Dunn's work, like most of the reform proposals themselves, focuses on the costs of campaigning for the presidency in general elections.

The politics of change is an important aspect of any reform effort. After examining the content of various reform plans, the study considers reactions of media personnel to the proposals advanced by other participants in the campaign process. It then assesses the likelihood that various reform proposals will accomplish the goals advanced by their proponents. Recommendations about the course of campaign finance reform are based on this analysis.

Mr. Dunn's is the second book in the Institution's current program of studies in presidential selection. The first was *Voting for President: The Electoral College and the American Political System*, by Wallace S. Sayre and Judith H. Parris, published in 1970. Other books will deal with such aspects of the presidential selection system as primaries, national convention management, and the impact of minor parties. A bipartisan national advisory panel of political activists and political journalists provides practical comment and other assistance in the development of the work. Although Mr. Dunn's research was undertaken prior to the appointment of the advisory panel, his book is included in the presidential selection series, where it naturally belongs.

Data for this work include personal interviews conducted with sixty-one individuals. Several of them, including political consultants and advertising agency personnel, had raised money and formulated the advertising strategy for the 1968 campaigns of Richard Nixon, Hubert Humphrey, and George Wallace. Finance and advertising specialists of the Democratic and Republican National Committees and the respective senatorial and congressional campaign committees for each party were interviewed, as were U.S. senators and representatives, members of their staffs, and members of the commerce committee in each house of Congress. Network executives in New York and Washington and spokesmen for the National Association of Broadcasters were also interviewed. In addition, a broadcast questionnaire was sent to 150 commercial television station general managers, 91 of whom responded. The author and the Institution are grateful to all of these people for their willingness to help.

The entire manuscript benefited from critical comments by Gilbert Y. Steiner, J. Carl Akins, Thomas E. Cronin, David Fleiss, Marjorie Girth, William Keech, Donald Matthews, Dan Mazmanian, Judith Parris, Ronald Randall, and several anonymous readers, and from skillful editing by Alice M. Carroll. Joan C. Culver prepared the index. William U. Hyden, Jr., served as research assistant for a portion of the project and Monica Kolasa and Michele Larrere served as secretaries for the project and as research aides.

Mr. Dunn conducted the research for this study as a research associate in Governmental Studies at Brookings. He is now associate professor of political science at the University of Georgia.

As always, the views expressed in this book are the author's, and do not necessarily reflect the views of the trustees, the officers, or other staff members of the Brookings Institution.

KERMIT GORDON
President

January 1972
Washington, D.C.

CONTENTS

TABLES

FINANCING PRESIDENTIAL CAMPAIGNS

☆

Chapter One

☆

ELECTIONS, CANDIDATES, AND CONTRIBUTORS

ELECTIONS are the key device in democratic government for regulating official decision making. When working properly, they assure that officeholders remain responsive to the greatest possible number of citizens.[1] In order to assure citizens the opportunity to judge the performance of officeholders, elections must occur periodically. The outcome of the last election coupled with anticipation of the next induces officials to produce an effort that can face the test of voter scrutiny. To exert their greatest impact, elections must be the final arbiter of power: they must determine who holds office. Any alternative source to which the prospective officeholder can appeal for the right to hold office—the military, for example—can constrict the responsiveness of elected officials to the public will, since the policy preferences of the alternative source may differ from those of the general electorate.

Elections must also provide voters with a choice, by presenting at least the alternative between the "ins" holding office and the "outs" who wish to be entrusted with office. Ideally, challengers should have a reasonably good chance of winning for the election to exert its most potent impact on policy. Without a challenge, the

1. See Robert A. Dahl, *A Preface to Democratic Theory* (University of Chicago Press, 1956); and William H. Riker, *Democracy in the United States*, 2nd ed. (Macmillan, 1965), pp. 35–83.

I

election would not determine who continued to hold office, thus diminishing its influence on the behavior of officeholders. Persons who wish to offer their ideas in the contest for office should have a reasonable opportunity to do so, thus broadening the scope of choice offered to voters.

Elections must, in addition, offer the greatest possible number of persons the right to vote; their votes must be calculated equally and the candidate receiving the greatest number of votes declared the victor. If suffrage were restricted, or if some votes counted more than others, the election would skew the responsiveness of the officeholder toward the preferences of the privileged voter, narrowing the group to whom officials felt responsible.

Finally, elections must help to educate voters about the alternatives that face them. Voting decisions based on imperfect information distort voters' preferences and thus the utility of elections as a mechanism for registering preferences.

Though few elections fully comply with all of these democratic requirements, any condition that thwarts any of them must be challenged. The widespread fear that campaign financing—so intimately involved in contesting for office—circumvents some of these requisites stems from a belief that present means of financing campaigns either make the political contest unequal or reduce the real alternatives presented to the voter for decision.

Does Money Win Elections?

No one can provide clear and easy answers to the question "Does money win elections?" Few candidates report the true costs of mounting campaigns. And officials frequently do not enforce the inadequate laws that govern finance reporting. The scant amount of reliable data on the cost of running for office in this country makes it possible only to speculate on the role money plays in electoral victories.

INGREDIENTS OF ELECTORAL SUCCESS

Campaign finance studies indicate that money does not guarantee electoral victory. One comprehensive study concluded that "no neat correlation is found between campaign expenditures and campaign results. Even if superiority in expenditures and success at the polls always ran together, the flow of funds to a candidate might simply reflect his prior popular appeal rather than create it. . . . Yet it is clear that under some conditions the use of funds can be decisive. And under others no amount of money spent by the loser could alter the outcome. . . . Financial outlays cannot guarantee victory in elections."[2] Other obviously influential factors in election victories are the voter's party identification, the campaign issues, the candidate's personality and the voters' reaction to it, the way in which campaign funds are managed, and incumbency, as well as a variety of intangibles.[3]

Party identification. Studies of voting behavior over the last thirty years have found that the stronger a voter's identification with a particular party, the more likely is he to choose the candidate of that party.[4] Thus, the candidate of the party that the higher percentage of voters identifies with possesses a built-in advantage in his quest for votes. He may have to spend less money to win than does his opponent. Nationally, since the late 1930s, more voters have identified with the Democratic party than with the Republican; Democratic candidates thus have a headstart over their Republican counterparts. The Democrat can win by "merely" holding all party-identifying Democrats. The Republican must hold all Republicans and then attract some independents and Democrats

2. Alexander Heard, *The Costs of Democracy* (University of North Carolina Press, 1960), p. 16.

3. For a candidate-centered view, see William Buchanan and Agnes Bird, *Money as a Campaign Resource: Tennessee Democratic Senatorial Primaries, 1948–1964* (Princeton, N.J.: Citizens' Research Foundation, 1966), pp. 8–12.

4. See Bernard R. Berelson, Paul F. Lazarsfeld, and William N. McPhee, *Voting* (University of Chicago Press, 1954), pp. 14–24; and Angus Campbell and others, *The American Voter* (Wiley, 1960), pp. 64–88, 120–45, 523–38.

(a considerably more difficult task) to win. This advantage partially compensates for the usually thinner purse with which the Democrats must finance national campaigns.

Issues. Issues do influence voting decisions.[5] During bad economic times, voters are apt to reject incumbents. Herbert Hoover could not have surmounted the public sentiment directed against him in 1932 even if the Republican party's funds had been unlimited. And the economic downturn during 1960 increased the prospects of Democrat John Kennedy. In 1952, voter disgust with the "unwinnable" Korean war worked to the advantage of Dwight Eisenhower, the "out" party candidate. Attitudes of voters toward the two parties as managers of government shift over the years. The current may run strongly enough to resist even the most elaborate and sophisticated campaign.

Attitudes toward candidates. Voters' attitudes about the personal attributes of a candidate and their beliefs about how he will behave in office often have an influence completely independent of the candidate's party label or his position on campaign issues. Dwight Eisenhower, for example, enjoyed high acclaim for his personal qualities; his challengers could do little to establish a more attractive image against such keen competition.[6] Candidates may find it difficult to overcome unattractive public images even though they spend lavishly to do so.

Although money cannot obliterate the influence of issues and candidates' party orientation on voting decisions, it can make a difference. The candidate who hires the most talented media personnel and buys the best television spots can tailor his image to gain favor with voters. Television advertising, some commentators believe, can actually falsify candidate characteristics and mis-

5. See Campbell and others, *The American Voter*, pp. 168–265.
6. For an argument that in 1952 Adlai Stevenson gained more from television in projecting personal traits than did Eisenhower—in part because of the lower base from which Stevenson began—see *The Influence of Television on the Election of 1952* (Oxford Research Associates, December 1954), p. 47 (cited by Heard, *The Costs of Democracy*, p. 26).

lead voters.[7] Some directors of media campaigns endorse a certain duplicity: "If [a candidate] has it, we project it. If he hasn't, we try to fudge it."[8] But others, like the adviser to a recent presidential candidate, question the wisdom of fudging: "I basically believe that you must be honest with television—that people will see through it when you aren't." And those who endorse some falsifying qualify their endorsement, "But we never strain the credibility of the viewer."[9] Candidates who can afford high-quality television advertising can thus create, within broad parameters, images that obscure their deficiencies. Depending on their opponents' ability to spend, and the public's reaction to their personality and issue stances, those candidates may find that lavish television expenditures may help, but not guarantee victory. In fact, Robert Goodman, a campaign adman, concluded after the 1970 congressional campaigns that "image-making can't run counter to strong national currents. TV can't overwhelm. It can only amplify."[10]

Efficiency of expenditures. One adviser to several presidential candidates suggested that "there is a tremendous waste of money in most campaigns." The uncertainty that pervades campaigns drives up costs; as a U.S. senator put it: "The trouble is that you never know the basic minimum that you need. You have to overspend just to make sure that you reach that point." No one knows precisely what needs to be done to win campaigns. The brevity of general election campaigns and of time to compensate for mistakes encourages the guideline "Better to be sure than to under-

7. See Joe McGinnis, *The Selling of the President 1968* (Trident, 1969), especially pp. 26–31; and Robert MacNeil, *The People Machine* (Harper & Row, 1968), especially pp. 126–62, 182–227.

8. Robert Goodman, in *Newsweek*, Oct. 19, 1970, p. 37.

9. *Ibid.*

10. *Newsweek*, Nov. 16, 1970, p. 77. Harold Mendelsohn and Irving Crespi, *Polls, Television, and the New Politics* (Scranton, Pa.: Chandler Publishing Co., 1970), pp. 247–56, point out that while television can focus attention, it rarely changes attitudes, largely because its messages interact with a lifetime of information previously made a part of the voter's experience. While this limits its potential impact, television can influence a voter's outlook toward a given candidate. And even if its conversion power is limited, its power to activate can be potent.

spend." Bumper stickers may make little difference; the frills of thousands of balloons may convert or activate few voters; but until the science of campaigning becomes more exact, candidates will spend regardless of the probable utility of a given expense in garnering votes. Some candidates by either accident or necessity may waste less than others.

An economic law common to many expenditures—after a certain point additional spending brings less return—also reduces the possibility of translating money into votes. One candidate, for example, may buy television time exposing his message to 100 percent of the television audience thirty times. Another may beam his message only twenty times to the same audience. But the total impact of the two may be much the same. With each additional commercial, the potential impact on the voter decreases; the viewer may, at some point, tire or even become disgruntled. Additional expenditures then may make more enemies than friends.[11]

Some campaign managers may allocate money more effectively than others. They may direct a higher percentage of their budgets to television (or other items that produce high payoffs). Or they may receive more for their money, as an advertising executive recently testified: "For approximately half the investment in television that Rockefeller made, we were able to buy some 95 percent of the [television] reaching frequency."[12]

Incumbency. One adage of politics holds that the incumbent enjoys many advantages over challengers. Whatever these advantages are, they accrue more readily to legislators than to executives, perhaps because the latter are frequently blamed by voters for poor government performance. Between 1954 and 1968, for

11. Although these are commonsense notions that guide political decisions, there has been little empirical validation of them—in part because exposure is difficult to measure. One study of English television viewers found that those who viewed ten or more "party election broadcasts" gained less knowledge during the campaign than those who viewed between four and nine such broadcasts but more knowledge than those who viewed three or less (Jay G. Blumler and Denis McQuail, *Television in Politics* [University of Chicago Press, 1969], pp. 161–62).

12. *The Campaign Broadcast Reform Act of 1969*, Hearings before the Senate Committee on Commerce, 91 Cong. 1 sess. (1969), p. 154.

example, only 8 percent of incumbent U.S. representatives and only 15 percent of incumbent U.S. senators contesting for reelection were defeated.[13] By contrast, in the 1950s and 1960s about 35 percent of incumbent governors attempting reelection were turned out by the voters.[14] Still, all of these groups have a better record for getting elected than do their challengers and, at least for these offices, incumbency can be counted an advantage. Incumbency provides several resources in the struggle for office. Visibility and identity with voters built up over the years of holding office are great assets, not readily purchased. The challenger must work vigorously to gain an identity, often making huge media expenditures. The additional advantages of incumbency include the public payroll, where many of the incumbent's campaign personnel can be lodged in one capacity or another. The frank permits congressional incumbents to mail literature free of charge,[15] spreading their campaign messages and solidifying their identity with the voter.

The amount that a challenger must spend to match these advantages of the incumbent is difficult to estimate and it varies by office. One writer has set the minimum value of incumbency (for the staff and government facilities it provides, the access to the mailing frank, and the lesser need to spend for advertising) at $16,000 for a U.S. senator or representative.[16]

Incumbency does, of course, include disadvantages. An incumbent's well-established identity with voters, for example, may limit his flexibility in tailoring his image to new voter demands.

13. Twentieth Century Fund, *Electing Congress* (New York: Twentieth Century Fund, 1970), p. 3.

14. J. Stephen Turett, "The Vulnerability of American Governors, 1900–1969," *Midwest Journal of Political Science*, Vol. 15 (February 1971), p. 118.

15. These mailings cannot contain literature that is overtly political, but in this instance "political" is usually defined rather narrowly and usually unenforced. An incumbent can continue mailings that outline his positions on the issues and contain statements he has inserted in the *Congressional Record*, and that perform services for his constituents.

16. David L. Rosenbloom, "Background Paper," in Twentieth Century Fund, *Electing Congress*, p. 36.

Voters may also identify him with unpopular programs or blame him for the troubles of the time—whatever they may be. At least two recent presidents (Truman and Johnson), despite the "advantages" of incumbency, have chosen not to test those advantages in a reelection campaign that many of their advisers thought they would lose.

Intangibles. Among the very elusive factors that can influence election results are the candidate's decision to emphasize one issue over another, or the scandal or sudden foreign crisis over which he has little control. An office seeker may find it difficult to adopt modern campaign techniques and be beaten by a skillful practitioner. Some candidates attract large cadres of talented staff while others, perhaps as able, do not inspire such loyalty. Strategies for allocating money or determining the blocs of states or groups of voters to emphasize can also affect the final outcome. These intangibles, though elusive, can determine the victor. All are related only casually, if at all, to the total expenditure for a campaign.

Money. It would be folly to argue that any single factor has a primary or central influence on election outcomes under all conditions. If more accurate information about campaign spending for a large number of elections were available, better guesses could be made about the edge (or its magnitude) that spending gives the victor. Spending linked with each variable—incumbency, party strength, the performance of ticket leaders, and so on—could be ranked by the importance of each combination to the final electoral victory. Obviously, money is among the factors that determine election victories; it is sometimes, but not always, the most important factor.

Despite the lack of any demonstrable effect of expenditures on victories in a large number of elections, no contestant is ready to cast money aside. Spending figures for presidential contests (the election for which figures are most nearly complete) during the last sixty years suggest that spending does not guarantee success; eight winners spent more than their opponents and seven spent less than the vanquished.[17] Four of the five most recent presidential winners, however, have outspent their opponents, and the fifth almost matched the spending of his challenger.[18] In addition, since World War II, Republican presidential candidates who have outspent their opponents by as much as 50 percent have won, as the following percentage excesses of the larger spender over the smaller show (asterisk denotes winning party):[19]

Candidate's party	1948	1952	1956	1960	1964	1968
Democratic	...*	...	...	10.1*	...*	...
Republican	3.6	71.0*	59.3*	...	2.9	49.3*

It may be, of course, that Republicans attract large amounts of money when their prospects for winning appear good. But the fact that so many recent winners have spent more than their opponents and that Republicans have managed to win in recent elections when they outspent the Democrats decisively may indicate that money is becoming more important in determining the victor than it was in the past. Moreover, candidates' increasing use of high-cost modern technology inevitably will make money more decisive in the future in determining election results.

Television. The most important campaign tool money can buy is television. Candidates are using it increasingly, adding huge costs to their campaigns. Contestants for statewide and national offices view the ability to finance television as a major ingredient of victory. Campaign managers demand a "basic minimum" exposure for candidates, without which they cannot win. One Humphrey adviser complained "the problem with the [1968]

17. Congressional Quarterly Service, *Politics in America 1945–68*, 3rd ed. (Washington: Congressional Quarterly Service, May 1969), p. 114. Congressional Quarterly's report of campaign expenditures is used here because it permits comparison over a longer period of time than do the expenditure sources cited later in this study. Since the Congressional Quarterly figures differ from those in the other sources for the 1956–68 period, computations based on them may differ somewhat also.

18. *Ibid.*

19. Computed from *ibid.*

Humphrey campaign was that we couldn't raise enough money to make even a minimal campaign." He did not define "minimal campaign." A U.S. senator partially clarified the notion: "If a candidate feels he can get his story across it takes a lot of pressure off. If I spent $200,000 on television and my opponent spent $400,000, I think I could beat him. But if I spent $100,000 and he spent $300,000 it might be a different story."

Poorly financed candidates in this era of modern campaigning are plagued with handicaps. Their inability to buy television time reduces their exposure; they will reach fewer people and do so less often than better financed candidates. They will buy less desirable time on programs reaching smaller audiences. Office seekers must purchase and pay for time in advance; the better financed will buy earliest and purchase the best spots; the poorly financed, even if they later raise funds, will find the "good" time gone.[20] And they will be less able to afford the sophisticated, and expensive, talent that can present the televised candidate most advantageously.

A poorly financed office seeker must exploit every opportunity for free time, and pay its "costs." He participates in local "talk" shows, often with inept hosts. Traveling to remote studios to reach small local audiences, he exhausts valuable time. And tiring schedules can never substitute for adequate exposure; candidates will find it increasingly difficult to replace modern techniques with workable, less costly means of reaching voters.

As winning turns more and more on who hires the most creative media personnel, finds the best (and most expensive) television time, and produces the most interesting commercials and programs, the potential impact of money on election victories looms larger and larger. "The impact of the media is the Democratic Party's major problem in the future," as Democratic National

20. Stations are required by Section 315 of the Communications Act to sell equal time to candidates for the same office. Although a one-minute spot at 8:00 on a Sunday evening, between two popular shows, may reach a larger audience than a spot at the same time on another evening, between two shows doing very poorly, the two times are equivalent according to the Section 315 standard.

Chairman Lawrence O'Brien, who managed the 1968 presidential campaign, sees it. "If we hadn't been able to match Nixon dollar for dollar in the last two weeks [of the 1968 campaign], this would have been the debacle everyone predicted. If you figure that by setting up a twenty-five-million-dollar budget, and making a game of who gets the best time slots and who hires the most creative media talent—and if you elect a President that way, what the Hell's the country coming to?"[21]

ACCESS TO THE ELECTION ARENA

Whether or not money determines campaign victors, it exerts an enormous influence on elections. High costs block (or control) access to the electoral arena. Potential candidates may choose not to run because they do not possess sufficient private resources to contest for office or fail to attract the financial support of the wealthy. Growing expenses impose requirements for holding office in addition to desire, experience, and qualification. High costs may also make it difficult for candidates to reach voters, thereby diminishing the level of information available to voters. As a result the wealthy who supply the necessary financing arbitrate who can contest for office; the wealthy who wish to contest for office have an advantage over others; and the expense of campaigning may reduce citizen access to information about elections.

As campaign costs soar the man of modest means must rely upon the well-to-do for campaign funding. Two current office-holders have noted how this can reduce the choices facing voters in elections:

MR. WRIGHT [a Texas congressman]: . . . But, Mr. Chairman, what good is all that if, in reality, the costs of elections and the difficulties of raising money from the little handful of fat cats who hold in their hands the power and the keys to public office are so restrictive that the public does not have much choice among those for whom it gets to cast its votes? . . .

THE CHAIRMAN [Senator Russell Long]: . . . Now, what you are say-

21. Quoted in Theodore H. White, *The Making of the President, 1968* (Atheneum, 1969), p. 417.

ing is that in many instances because of the problems of financing a campaign, the public oftentimes does not really get much choice. Both candidates pretty well have to be acceptable to the small percentage of people who are paying the campaign expenses of those candidates in any event.[22]

The nonwealthy man desiring to contest for office must appeal to the wealthy for funds. Many aspirants may not meet whatever set of criteria the wealthy choose to impose. This adds an undesirable component to the electoral process, for voters do not participate in this exercise. By giving the wealthy veto power over who may contest, high campaign costs grant them greater influence than other voters have in determining who achieves office.

The point is dramatically illustrated by Eugene Nickerson's withdrawal from the 1970 New York State Democratic gubernatorial primary campaign. Nickerson was a serious candidate who had been endorsed by the party's large liberal segment, the New Democratic Coalition. He had received enough support from the Democratic State Committee to be guaranteed a place on the state primary election ballot. But he did not run in the primary because, he said, he could not raise enough money to campaign against former U.N. Ambassador Arthur Goldberg and Howard Samuels: "I've decided not to continue as a candidate for the Democratic nomination for Governor. I made that decision, basically because we could not raise sufficient funds to continue the effort. . . . Goldberg's entry dried up resources and funds."[23] Before dropping out, Nickerson had raised perhaps $300,000 of a $750,-000 primary campaign budget.

As campaign costs increase, men with personal fortunes have an

22. *Political Campaign Financing Proposals*, Hearings before the Senate Committee on Finance, 90 Cong. 1 sess. (1967), pp. 267–68. Several scholars have found that since the 1930s the two major parties have attracted financing from different groups. The most notable distinction is that Republicans draw funds disproportionately from business, banking, and insurance while the Democrats rely heavily upon labor. See, for example, Heard, *The Costs of Democracy*, pp. 95–141, 168–211. Little evidence has thus far been collected on the differences, of specific ideological and policy attitudes, between those who contribute and those who do not.

23. *New York Times*, April 16, 1970.

edge over those with no fortunes. Howard Samuels, for example, stayed in the New York campaign that Eugene Nickerson abandoned. And Representative Bertram Podell is quoted as saying: "When I ran for Congress, the first question asked me was whether I could finance my own campaign. If I had said 'no, I cannot,' I would not have been the candidate. When you mention candidates for public office, you are only mentioning men of affluence."[24] Indeed, a student of campaign finance found that the Rockefeller fortune provided much of the wherewithal used by at least one campaign committee supporting Governor Nelson Rockefeller in his bid for the Republican presidential nomination in 1968: "Receipts totalled $1,840,627, and expenditures were in an identical amount. Mrs. Martha Baird Rockefeller, Nelson's stepmother, contributed a total of $1,482,625 in eight separate amounts ranging from $425,000 on June 6 to $10,000 on September 18. Nelson gave $350,000 on August 15, and Laurance S. Rockefeller gave a total of $2,000 in two contributions. The remainder was made up in contributions of outsiders ranging from 25 cents to $5,000."[25]

High campaign costs block candidate access to the electoral arena. They bar men of talent who could make constructive contributions. And they make it impossible for groups without money to enter the electoral arena to offer their ideas in competition with those who can afford the price of admission.

When inadequate funding prevents a candidate from taking his case to the people, the base of information on which citizens make their decisions is affected. Voters may reject the candidate's case not on its merits, but because he cannot convey his message to as many as possible. Democratic elections further require that alternatives be offered for voter choice. Candidates must vigorously present these alternatives to insure voter awareness of them. If

24. "Campaign Spending in the 1968 Elections," *Congressional Quarterly Weekly Report*, Vol. 27 (Dec. 5, 1969), p. 2434.

25. Herbert E. Alexander, "Financing Parties and Campaigns in 1968: A Preliminary Report" (paper delivered at the 1969 meeting of the American Political Science Association; processed), p. 10.

adequate financing prevents a candidate from fulfilling his obligation to educate, the ideal electoral process breaks down. The more imperfect the information the voters receive, the less informed their choices among alternatives. Once again, campaign financing disturbs the smooth functioning of democratic elections.

Does Money Affect Policy Decisions?

Americans often view public policy making as a sordid process where the wealthy control elected officials. Corruption in high places—influence peddling, bribery, illegal contributions—does occur, but its reputation for moving the wheels of government is far more potent than its performance.[26] For money twists policy making in a considerably more subtle fashion, sometimes more broadly, sometimes less so, than does the venal corruption of popular hearsay.

THE LIMITS OF MONEY

The obvious use of money to affect the policy-making process is limited by the public norms that govern giving and receiving. In their most visible form, those norms are enforceable through public laws. The constraints are reenforced on the one hand by officials' inclination to view giving as unrelated to policy making, and on the other by donors' limited choice of officeholders, actual or potential, on whom to work their will.

Public norms. Public norms proscribe officials dancing to the tune of fat cats who seek to influence public policy. The various corrupt practices acts that prohibit bribery and campaign contributions by groups that might benefit from public favor rarely work, but they do represent efforts to reduce the influence of money.

Considerably more potent barriers to the direct translation of money into policy decisions are officials' perceptions of public

26. Such beliefs nevertheless diminish confidence in the democratic policy-making process.

expectations. Policy makers know that the public views suspiciously any exchange of money. They consequently avoid appearing to be the willing wards of the wealthy.

Candidates wishing to minimize their obligations frequently limit their donors' largess. As a congressman's aide explained: "When you have four people each contributing $20,000 per year, it might be hard to tell any one of them no. But we limit our contributions. No individual can give over $250." Presumably a large base of small givers limits an official's obligation to any one and frees him to act in the "public interest" as he sees it.

Those obligations can also be reduced if the donors are unidentified. An adviser to many presidential aspirants explained that "the basic way a candidate handles money is that he lets someone else handle it for him. He may not want to know where the money comes from." The fetters of obligations implicit in the acceptance of contributions are thus loosened. Potential donors find it difficult to make themselves (and their policy interests) known to candidates. One savvy campaign adviser provided the answer to their dilemma: "The smart ones handle this by telling the candidate that he wants to contribute. The candidate will then tell him who to see. That way you can be sure that the candidate knows you have contributed."

A time-honored practice of candidates in accepting contributions is to make no explicit promises. A campaign veteran commented: "I've actually had very few people who come to me wanting to give on a quid pro quo basis. I think that the American people would be surprised about how rarely this occurs. It happens very, very rarely. And when it does the guy who tries it is usually so naïve that you feel sorry for him." A long-time congressman met the problem in the following way: "I've never, in all my years in politics, had but one man who approached me, reminded me of his contribution, and asked me to do something. I immediately went to the bank, borrowed the money, and gave him back his contribution." Officials do not want it to appear that their vote or influence is for sale; that smacks of bribery and would no doubt be viewed as such if it became public. Americans may not adequately finance campaigns but they are not willing to elect officials who appear to be for sale to the highest bidder. Arranging quid pro quo deals may also be illegal since some laws proscribe the direct exchange of money in influence peddling d vote buying and selling.

Well-advised donors therefore avoid asking for explicit commitments in return for contributions. The finance director of a national campaign described the at best uncouth, at worst illegal, donation: "Then there is . . . the special interest money. The trucking industry, beer, liquor, name anyone you want. They sometimes come in because they want to influence a contract, an appointment, or perhaps get you to come out for a specific policy. They are often very forthright about it. I tell these people quite frankly that if there are quicker ways to Leavenworth [the federal prison], I don't know about them." To contribute effectively, donors must be more subtle, indirect, and implicit. Their ability to elicit promises, and to turn money directly into policy influence, is thus limited.

Candidates, reflecting public norms, refuse money from certain sources: a convicted racketeer, a person with unsavory business connections, and the like are all taboo. The public will not impute selfless motives, "civic pride," or good government goals to such contributors. And candidates consequently avoid such irreputable sources because the mere acceptance of their money, in the public view, constitutes an onerous obligation. The more circuitous route, often through respected conduits, that these contributions must take increases the possibility that the policy motive behind the money will become lost in the transaction.

Contributors' interests. Candidates often diminish their policy obligations to contributors by divorcing their benefactors' motives from policy goals. Some people, they assume, give for social reasons, to appear to be on close terms with a senator, a congressman, or the President. Contributors "show off" these friends by inviting them to social functions, and the candidate or official usually accepts. Gossip about the occasion spreads word of the friendship far and wide, and the giver seldom remains quiet about such social catches. A senator's aide commented that "a good many [social givers] want nothing else but for the Senator to attend their son's Bar Mitzvah." And many people crave invitations to White House dinners: "Most of these people [contributors] want an invitation to a White House Dinner, some back slapping, and some proof that they are the President's friend." Such contributions impose relatively painless obligations on the candidate, and repaying them is relatively easy, even enjoyable for some. Best of all, they require no policy commitments.

Candidates have a limited sense of obligation to those who seem to give as a civic duty. One party official stated: "I think that most people give money because they believe that they have a civic obligation to do so. They know that campaigning is important to a democracy, that it costs money, and that they can help." Their satisfaction presumably derives from acting responsibly as citizens. They expect no favors in return. A large number of contributors (although not necessarily a large percentage of contributions) doubtless fall primarily into this category. They diminish the policy obligations the candidate incurs in financing his campaign. They also provide the candidate some psychological comfort, a comfort that he can inflate out of all proportion to the size of this group.

Givers also contribute as a means of participating, directly or vicariously, in a campaign. One party official felt that the "biggest givers give because of the excitement of a campaign. They want to be a part of it and their money is a ticket. Sometimes they know it makes something possible [that is vital to the campaign]." One reward for these backers is to "let them ride a couple of stops" when there is room on the campaign plane for them. A senator commented: "There are an awful lot of rich folks around who want something to do with their money. They need to participate. So they contribute to a candidate in much the same way, and with much the same motivation, as someone would bet on a racehorse."

Candidates like to believe many contributions are made for this reason, for they impose no policy-related obligations.

Givers, of course, contribute to campaigns for an amalgam of reasons; categorizing them may imply an easy divisibility of goals that does not actually exist. But it does permit examining the extent to which each goal (or the candidate's perception if it) constrains the policy-related actions of officials. Candidates perceive many contributors' goals as free of policy expectations, thus setting no bounds on later policy choices.[27] Even these persons, however, are not apt to contribute to candidates whose broad policy stances are at odds with their own goals.

Officials' leverage. Public officials do not form blank slates upon which contributors can write any message they wish. An office-holder who decides to oppose the policy interests of large contributors can do so. But he does not do so lightly, as a congressional aide indicated in relating how his boss called in several large contributors "and told them they were wrong on the matter and that he was going against them. He had no hesitancy whatsoever in doing it." No official, regardless of the extent of his "hesitancy," likes to tell the friends who support him financially that he has decided to oppose their position. He does it only when he must. The fact that he feels he must call them in to explain indicates something of the impact of money on policy decisions.

An official can, of course, agree with his benefactors in public while working privately to thwart their policy interests. The intricate, labyrinthine American policy process assists him in doing this. He may, for example, after assuring his benefactors that he supports a position near and dear to their hearts, ask the subcommittee chairman who has jurisdiction over the matter to "sit" on the bill because he does not want to take a public position

27. For an excellent discussion of the motivation of contributors, see Heard, *The Costs of Democracy*, pp. 68–94. He cautions against analyzing motivations in selfish or nonselfish categories since all motivations serve certain needs or aspirations (pp. 72–74). His point is well taken. Hence the attempt to analyze the extent to which party and public officials' (as opposed to givers') perceptions of contributions are viewed as policy related.

on it. Or he may vote for promising new programs on the floor of the legislature but see members of the appropriations committee privately and ask them to withhold funds that would be necessary to start the new program.[28]

Officeholders may calculate that they can disagree with large contributors as long as they do not become less attractive to donors than their potential opponents. A person active in both the soliciting and giving ends of campaign financing commented: "You can't really persuade a guy to go with you by threatening to cut off his money. He usually thinks you didn't give him enough in the first place. And he may be better than any potential opponent." And another cynic succinctly stated the dilemma facing many contributors: "It's better to have half-a-friend than an enemy."

THE POWER OF GIVING

Candidates cannot raise all the money they need from persons who want them to attend their daughter's wedding or their son's Bar Mitzvah. Wheedling contributions by going through "so much sham to make [donors] think that they are indeed influential," as one party official put it, does not always produce enough money. People giving solely out of a sense of civic duty do not constitute a vast throng. Candidates must also rely on gifts from those who wish to advance policy preferences or ideological commitments. Such money can affect policy decisions primarily by providing the contributors access to officials and forcing candidates to make implicit commitments.

Access to officeholders. Candidates, fund raisers, campaign advisers, and persons close to them universally agree that contributors improve their access to elected officials through the mere act of giving to candidates. "The art of politics is getting yourself known," as a national campaign manager commented. "People

---

28. Of course, the opposite can also occur. Officials can make their public activity appear to be serving the "public interest" while using the techniques just described to serve "private interests" in important ways that may be crucial to them.

who are known can get inside doors much more quickly. If you had told me when you wanted in or came in that you had contributed $25,000 to the ———— campaign, I would have stood up and taken notice. It's natural to do that. Contributions can certainly assist efforts to get yourself known."

Once a person becomes "known," he finds arranging appointments with busy officials somewhat easier. One senator admitted "letting some people through the door who wouldn't otherwise get through if they weren't contributors." Another confessed: "Someone from the 'walnut' lobby called me up the other day and wanted to see me about import quotas. I told him, 'Hell no, I don't want to see you!' I suppose, in all honesty, that if they had contributed— and they hadn't—I would have felt it necessary to see him." An adviser to several presidential candidates summed up the relationship between giving and access: "The very least that a contributor expects his contribution to do is to get him access the next time he has a problem he wants to take up with the officeholder."

Knowing the right people and being able to reach them is prerequisite to influencing American policy outcomes. David Truman's classic discussion of access called it the "basic objective" of interest groups.[29] Although persuading unsympathetic officials is usually difficult for even the most artful salesman, the petitioner granted a hearing by the officeholder can at least make his case in person. The adroit claimant can effectively demonstrate what he wants and why he wants it—often through vivid personal illustrations. He has a great edge over others, winning victory by default if other sides of the issue never enter the decision maker's calculations. And competing claims may never be as vivid or have as great an impact as those presented in face-to-face communication. As the demand for the time of officials intensifies, access becomes more and more valuable. Most persons find it difficult to arrange appointments with elected officials, particularly to talk about policy matters. Thus any tool that facilitates access assumes great value.

29. David R. Truman, *The Governmental Process* (Knopf, 1951), p. 264; see also pp. 264–70, 321–51.

Party leaders and officeholders rush to discount that value. A senator's aide asserted: "If a person gives money it makes it possible for him to get directly to the Senator. For some people, this is important. They think that's what it takes to get things done. But anyone can get to the staffer, and these people actually get the work done." Staff assistants do handle the details of a top official's work. Many offices facilitate appointments with staff members, who train themselves to grant polite hearings to any and all. But staffers work most persistently and enthusiastically on those matters their boss is interested in. They may attempt to interest him in matters that an outsider brings to their attention. But the claimant going through a staff member may find that his petition stops there, never to be seen or heard by the official.

Implicit commitments. The implicit commitments a candidate makes to raise money for his campaign are the most potent channel for influencing policy making. Most candidates solicit money on the basis of their prior public performance. Seekers of major office have communicated their overarching positions on numerous matters: labor-management relations, government regulation, budgetary levels and priorities. A candidate's stance on these and other matters tells potential contributors whether he be friend or foe.

Solicitation by either the office seeker or his staff implicitly promises a sympathetic response to matters of interest to the giver arising during the candidate's term of office. But the transaction is subtle, as a veteran campaign manager makes clear: "I don't think there are often deals where money is exchanged for votes. But it is usually vague. When a candidate tells contributors 'You know you have a friend in Washington,' what does he mean? There's a good deal of this. It's vague. And intelligent people keep it that way."

To what extent then does a candidate's solicitation and acceptance of money obligate him to follow the policy positions of a contributor? Because the understanding is tacit, the office seeker has some latitude in his interpretation. But the donor may feel the commitment is firmer or more specific than the candidate does.

Later on, the candidate-become-official may resent any attempts at retribution or intimations that he owes specific favors in return for the contribution—in part because of the public norms that govern contributions. But officials usually honor commitments to the contributor's general interests and will support them in specific cases when they can.

Money thus buys a contributor a foot in the door and usually assures a sympathetic hearing. But it cannot assure that the official will decide exactly as the contributor would like. Contributions seldom buy specific commitments because no candidate wants to present the impression that he can be bought; and he wants some latitude in appraising all the factors as he makes decisions.

Contributors who successfully ply this trade recognize the key elements of the process. It is legitimate to contribute for policy ends, for a good many people do: "Very few people contribute out of the goodness of their hearts. They want a little blood in return," according to a veteran campaign manager. But if the donor is not to be disappointed, his policy expectations must be general and broad: "People often expect favors for giving. But of the number which do, I've seen the same number disappointed when they attempted to get the favor they felt they were entitled to," said one party official. Unless a giver has a very good bargaining position with a candidate, he must never expect specific promises. Implicit, broad, tacit, general, vague—these best sum up the characteristics of campaign giving and getting.

Implicit commitments are not necessarily less troublesome than explicit ones; they can also lock officials into policy positions. How can the candidate-become-official extricate himself from the clutching promises of friendship if he should happen to change his mind while in office? This is not a hypothetical possibility—public office can provide a powerful education experience. The state legislator who becomes a congressman might find the view from Washington different from that back home. He might while touring impoverished areas develop a view that would support greater government economic activity or stricter regulation of certain types of business than he would have supported when first elected to office.

Or the ardent pro-labor activist might develop the belief that the labor movement had become fat and complacent and was no longer the vigorous, idealistic crusader for human achievement that it once was. A party pro aptly stated: "The bad thing about requiring so much money is that it eventually locks people into positions. They won't admit it and most can get out of it if they want to. But they solicit money on grounds that they have been friends with certain people while in public life. They just don't take money from people they oppose. But what happens if they want to change their positions? It becomes increasingly harder to do."

Once an official establishes a successful formula for raising the funds necessary for campaigning, he tampers with the formula reluctantly. He usually prefers to leave well-enough alone and thereby avoid the agonizing and uncertain process of building a new coalition of contributors. He may also feel bound by his old commitments. Campaign soliciting methods thus reduce the flexibility with which officials can respond to new conditions (that might require new policy orientations) or to their own changed perspectives about policy.

This "locking-in" is not necessarily manifest to officials. The ingenious human mind usually convinces itself that the good, pure, and beautiful motivate almost everything it does. Public officials usually do not want to admit (to others or themselves) that financial calculations even indirectly affect policy activity. The calculations may indeed be subconscious because by second nature most elected officials adeptly calculate the political risks and implications of most of their activities. Though they may not always consciously relate their decisions to their ability to raise money, their protests that money never locks them into positions are suspect.

Current methods of financing campaigns raise the possibility that candidates will put financial requirements above policy commitment. The principal goal of most candidates is to be elected. The expense frequently is great, and the need to raise funds may compromise policy principles.

The candidate who contests a seat for the first time must often challenge the incumbent, or someone closely allied with him, who over the years has built an alliance of contributors. The challenger must cast about for uncommitted money. He may bend his commitments in the process. He issues position papers or makes public statements designed to appeal to the interests of those with uncommitted money. He assures people in private that they have a friend in him. He thus implicitly commits himself—perhaps more firmly than the candidate enjoying a long-term alliance—to policy positions that lock him in to positions that can influence his activity far beyond his first election victory.

During a campaign a candidate may find that his funds are not adequate. A U.S. senator commented, "Now if I wanted to, it would be easy to raise money from the big ———— and ————— [groups with business before his economically important committee]. But then it wouldn't be any fun to be a United States Senator. My hands would be tied on a lot of matters that I care a great deal about." Any senator might become considerably more practical if he discovered during a campaign that he needed money to match his opponent's efforts in order to stay in the Senate. Senator Russell Long once illustrated how the needs of a campaign can alter perspectives: "I have seen men start out running for Governor with the firm intention of promising nothing. Coming down the stretch, I have seen them making commitments that it made me sick to see. They did it because they could not pay for radio and television. Their sign boards were taken down, and the only way they could cross that finish line and make a respectable showing was to make promises they did not want to make, such as promising the highway contractors who the contract would be given to; promising the insurance companies who the insurance commissioner would be."[30]

Present methods of campaign financing may unfairly exclude some ideas from the electoral contest and therefore from the halls of government. Persons of little means whose ideas are contrary to those of the wealthy cannot run for office. The economic barrier

30. *Political Campaign Financing Proposals*, Hearings, p. 178.

of campaign financing thus closes election to office to those who would by electing "friends" to office seek more direct representation of their ideas. Friends helping friends is not dishonorable. But "friends" without money cannot gain sympathetic representation in the policy-making process by helping "friends" who wish to contest for office but cannot pay high campaign costs.

This flaw directly contradicts popular and theoretical concepts of democratic government. A government that bases its legitimate authority on the "consent of the governed" cannot long maintain its legitimacy when the money behind an idea rather than its merit determines its chance to receive a fair hearing. No matter how subtle or implicit the process, money expedites the sympathetic reception of ideas. As the process becomes increasingly visible, fewer accept the sources of authority for the government system. One U.S. senator, explaining his interest in campaign finance legislation, stated: "The very integrity of the system is at stake. People have less confidence in the system than they have ever had. I think that one of the prime reasons is the distrust which is a part of the present way of financing elections." The current challenge to the authority structure occurs at the very time when campaign costs are increasing rapidly and when money is becoming a more central factor in determining election outcomes than ever before.

Finally, present financing methods increase pressure on candidates to raise the additional money required to campaign and thereby intensify their need to make implicit commitments. Those who become officials may thus find their hands tied on an ever widening area of policy decisions, with a concomitant reduction of the areas in which they have some latitude.

☆

Chapter Two

☆

THE COST OF
MODERN CAMPAIGNING

SINCE THE first settlers arrived at Jamestown and Plymouth Rock, Americans have campaigned for public office. By the 1820s the prototype of American elections had developed: candidates campaigning for office among a widely franchised electorate (at least as compared with earlier times) using several time-honored techniques—the stump, the handshake, shoeleather, and a dash of whiskey or cider on the side. These techniques were relatively cheap. Many successful candidates financed campaigns with modest amounts—Abraham Lincoln spent only 75 cents in his first successful race for the House of Representatives.[1]

But contesting for office has changed drastically since those simple, rustic days. Elected leaders no longer represent small, personalized constituencies. When George Washington presided over a nation of 4 million people, each member of the House of Representatives represented 30,000 persons. That number has grown to 500,000 in a nation of over 200 million people.

At the same time that constituencies have become depersonalized, competition for the attention of the citizen has increased. Man's surroundings buzz with a diversity of entertainment and

1. Statement of Russell D. Hemenway, director of National Committee for an Effective Congress, in *Campaign Broadcast Reform Act of 1969*, Hearings before the Senate Committee on Commerce, 91 Cong. 1 sess. (1969), p. 51.

occupations, and men's mobility and activities have made the candidate's coming to town (or the urban clubhouse spate of activities) an antiquated competitor for the most exciting show running.

Candidates have thus turned to new techniques to identify themselves and their messages to large numbers of voters. Representative Jim Wright, campaigning for the U.S. Senate in Texas, discovered the futility of using past practices in present campaigns. He had assumed "that a determined man in good health could make up by prodigious personal effort what he lacked in finances." After a grueling schedule of personal appearances and handshaking he concluded that "it was like trying to siphon off the Gulf of Mexico with an eyedropper. For there were then ten million people in Texas; if I worked sixteen hours a day and wasted no time, it would have taken me some twenty-eight years to talk for one minute with every citizen in the State."[2]

Television leads the rapidly expanding array of technological tools for campaigning. The elaborate public opinion polls, talented writers and producers, sophisticated consultants, and costly computers[3] associated with campaigning are employed primarily to insure the effective use of television. Candidates have their best chance to penetrate the consciousness of most citizens through television. "It's the only media people pay attention to. Exposure is what is important. And the only way to get it is through television," was the thought of one advertising agency veteran of several campaigns. Television's ability to reach people supplies its strength as a campaign tool. In 1950 only 3.8 million or 9 percent of U.S. households had television. That number had grown to 71 percent by 1956, and by 1968, 57 million, or 95 percent of all, households had television sets.[4] According to a Nielsen report, the television set in the average home in 1968 was in use forty-three

---

2. Jim Wright, "Clean Money for Congress," *Harper's Magazine*, April 1967, pp. 100–01.

3. See Dan Nimmo, *The Political Persuaders: The Techniques of Modern Election Campaigns* (Prentice-Hall, 1970); and James M. Perry, *The New Politics* (New York: Clarkson N. Potter, 1968).

4. *Nielsen TV 1969* (Chicago: A. C. Nielsen Co., 1969), p. 10.

hours a week—over six hours a day. For twenty-three of those hours the "man of the house" was watching; the "woman of the house" watched for almost thirty hours a week.[5] The Nielsen figures are slightly higher than the median determined by a 1968 Roper survey: Americans watch television two hours and forty-seven minutes a day.[6] All studies agree that Americans spend more time in watching television (or at least in sitting in front of the television set) than in any other activity except work and sleep. It is thus little wonder that candidates for public office seek to harness this powerful tool in their efforts to identify themselves to voters.

But getting on television is just half of the story. Unless a candidate exploits his television appearances by sophisticated programing, he may lose more than he gains. Former Vice President Hubert Humphrey, plagued by inadequate financing throughout his two quests for the presidency, is the most dramatic example of the uselessness of exposure without adequate professional production. In the 1960 West Virginia primary he could buy statewide television hook-ups for half-hour periods at the low price of $750. Humphrey raised even this small amount with difficulty, and on at least one occasion, according to Theodore H. White, paid for the time with a personal check. "Such a grocery-money check buys time only—it does not buy the production, the preparation, the care a major television manipulation of the public requires."[7] White relates the fiasco of a Humphrey telethon that degenerated into an incomprehensible jumble, ranging from old ladies telling him to "git out" to friendly farmers welcoming him back.[8] A candidate who captures an audience with television must make the best of the moment. If his image and the message he conveys make a negative impression on the audience, they are less helpful than no appearance at all.

5. *Ibid.*, pp. 14–15.

6. Burns W. Roper, *A Ten-Year View of Public Attitudes Toward Television and Other Mass Media 1959–1968* (New York: Television Information Office, 1969), p. 6.

7. Theodore H. White, *The Making of the President 1960* (Antheneum, 1961), p. 110.

8. *Ibid.*, pp. 110–12.

This is why the role of the political consultant—the person who orchestrates modern technology for the candidate—is growing. Polls for the candidates identify areas of potential strength and weakness, both in image and issue, and suggest campaign themes to incorporate into television advertising. They also pinpoint groups or geographical areas where voters may be won over and others where campaigning or advertising would be wasted. Computers supply analyses of polling results and past strengths of a candidate or party that can be used to further refine campaign appeals and strategy.[9]

Specialists competing with each other on behalf of their candidates are characteristic of the modern campaign. Media specialists create cleverly designed commercials, elaborately contrived telethons, and "documentary" biographies to replace the thirty-minute straight talk presentation. Skilled producers vie with each other to produce attractive film that will entertain viewers and dispense messages advantageous to the candidate. Talented media buyers compete for twenty-, thirty-, and sixty-second spots that will reach the most viewers or a particular type of viewer that modern demographic rating services have found watching particular programs. Deft scriptwriters, in consultation with poll analysts, labor to fashion arresting messages that convey to the enraptured (or captured?) viewer the proper sentiments about the candidate. All help the candidate to make the most effective (from his perspective) possible use of television.

Modern technology permits candidates to communicate with voters as they become more difficult to reach in an increasingly complex society. In a sense, television substitutes for the face-to-face contact of a former time, when candidates could gain some understanding of constituent preferences and citizens some measure of the contestants. Though the "artificial" modern-day technological "interaction" may be criticized, this more populous and more complex age requires such a means of voter-candidate communication if any is to occur at all.

9. Some candidates also use computers to write "personal" letters stressing matters of interest to particular groups of voters.

Modern technology vastly increases campaign costs. Computers, polls, consultants, broadcasting time, and production costs are expensive investments, and growing campaign expenditures over the past several national election years reflect this increased cost.

Growth in Campaign Costs

It is difficult to evaluate growth in campaign costs because of the serious gaps in campaign finance reporting. The most comprehensive figures available chart the expenditures of national level committees (those spending in two or more states) usually in support of presidential and vice presidential candidates during the general election period. Even at this level many expenses remain unreported.[10] Transfers between committees, expenditures by committees operating independently (usually in a single state) from national committees, or expenditures made by national committees on local contests further shroud the true cost of electing the president and vice president. The expense reports filed with the Clerk of the House of Representatives are the best source of information on national campaign expenses, even though they are incomplete.

Data compiled from these reports show that direct presidential campaign expenditures at the national level more than tripled between the national elections of 1956 and 1968 (see Table 1). The increase in costs was greatest between 1964 and 1968, as the following percentages indicate:

	1956–60	*1960–64*	*1964–68*	*1956–68*
Increase in campaign costs	56.4	23.8	81.0	250.3

10. Some national committees also support U.S. Senate and House candidates. National level committees usually operate as adjuncts of their party's national committee. In 1964 national Democratic committees included Americans Abroad for Johnson, Citizens for Johnson-Humphrey, Veterans for Johnson-Humphrey, and so on. Republican counterparts included Brothers for Goldwater, National Federation of Republican Women, Solid South Speaks for Goldwater, and so forth.

TABLE 1. Presidential Campaign Expenditures at the National Level, 1956–68

In dollars

Item	1956	1960	1964	1968
Total direct expenditures[a]	13,732,000	21,474,000	26,580,000	48,119,000
Republican committees	7,795,000	10,128,000	16,024,000	25,422,000
Democratic committees	4,802,000	9,797,000	8,757,000	11,593,000
Labor committees	541,000	843,000	725,000	1,872,000
American Independent committees	...	...	...	7,223,000
Miscellaneous committees	594,000	706,000	1,074,000	2,009,000
Expenditure per potential voter[b]	0.13	0.20	0.24	0.41
Broadcast expenditures[c]	4,723,147	d	11,081,565	20,376,595
For television	3,669,897	d	8,895,613	14,637,750
Networks	2,865,633[e]	d	3,807,011[f]	7,362,240
Spots	386,051	d	n.a.	3,518,456
Programs	2,124,006	d	n.a.	3,843,784
Stations	804,264	d	5,088,602	7,275,510
For Radio	1,053,250	d	2,185,952[f,g]	5,738,845
Networks	318,261	d	119,365	662,674
Stations	734,989	d	2,066,587	5,076,171

Sources: *1956 General Election Campaigns,* Report of the Subcommittee on Privileges and Elections to the Senate Committee on Rules and Administration, 85 Cong. 1 sess (1957), Exhibit 4, p. 41, Exhibit 24, pp. 4, 14 (cited hereafter as Gore Committee Report). Herbert E. Alexander, *Financing the 1960 Election* (Princeton, N.J.: Citizens' Research Foundation, 1962), p. 10; *Financing the 1964 Election* (Citizens' Research Foundation, 1966), p. 8; *Financing the 1968 Election* (Heath Lexington, 1971), pp. 117–24. Federal Communications Commission (FCC), *Survey of Political Broadcasting, 1964,* Tables 3, 9A, 22A; and *Survey of Political Broadcasting, 1968,* Tables 5, 9, 20.

n.a. Not available.

a. Includes known debts; excludes transfers to candidates and committees below the national level. Figures for 1956 are for Jan. 1 through Nov. 30, for other years for Jan. 1 through Dec. 31.

b. Based on estimated voting age population (U.S. Bureau of the Census, *Statistical Abstract of the United States, 1969,* p. 368).

c. Figures for 1956 are for Sept. 1 to election day, for other years for the general election period.

d. Figures not collected separately for the presidential campaign by the FCC in 1960.

e. Total is greater than the sum of costs for spots and programs because it includes production and preemption charges.

f. Figure is for network spending by all candidates, but those below the presidential level spend little on network television.

g. Figures include no FM stations programed separately from AM stations.

In the same period, general election campaign expenditures by all candidates stopped just short of doubling (see Table 2).

The number of potential voters in the United States has also grown since 1956, and candidates have spent more in an effort to reach them (Table 1). Both national campaign costs and the expenditure per potential voter tripled between 1956 and 1968, as Figure 1 shows. Spending per voter almost doubled in the eight-year period between 1956 and 1964 and more than doubled between 1960 and 1968. This indicates that total costs have consistently increased regardless of serious third-party challenges (spending per potential voter would have increased to 35 cents in

TABLE 2. Election Campaign Expenditures by All Candidates, 1956–68

In dollars

Item	1956	1960	1964	1968
Estimated total, all candidates[a]	155,000,000	175,000,000	200,000,000	300,000,000
Broadcast expenditures[b]	9,907,006	14,195,278	24,603,989	40,403,498
For television	6,685,709	10,052,322	17,496,405	27,087,027
Networks	2,930,514[c]	2,927,235	3,807,011	7,362,240
Spots	386,051	n.a.	n.a.	3,518,456
Programs	2,171,808	n.a.	n.a.	3,843,784
Stations	3,755,195[c]	7,125,087	13,689,394	19,724,787
Spots	1,917,759	n.a.	10,608,579	17,459,730
Programs	1,521,079	n.a.	3,080,815	2,265,057
For radio	3,221,297	4,142,956	7,107,584[d]	13,316,471
Networks	320,940	78,867	119,365	662,674
Stations	2,900,357	4,064,089	6,988,219	12,653,797

Sources: Gore Committee Report, Exhibit 24, pp. 1, 4, 14. Alexander, *Financing the 1960 Election*, p. 12; *Financing the 1964 Election*, p. 13. Herbert E. Alexander, "Financing Parties and Campaigns in 1968: A Preliminary Report" (paper presented at the 1969 meeting of the American Political Science Association). Alexander Heard, *The Costs of Democracy* (University of North Carolina Press, 1960), p. 8. FCC, *Survey of Political Broadcasting, 1960*, Table 1; *1964*, Tables 1, 9; *1968*, Tables 3, 5, 8.

n.a. Not available.

a. Figures are for Jan. 1 through Dec. 31.

b. Figures for 1956 and 1960 are for Sept. 1 to general election date, for 1964 and 1968 for the general election period.

c. Total is greater than the sum of costs for spots and programs because it includes production and preemption charges.

d. Figures include no FM stations programed separately from AM stations.

FIGURE I. Increases in Expenditures for Presidential and All
Campaigns and in Expenditures per Potential Voter, 1956–68

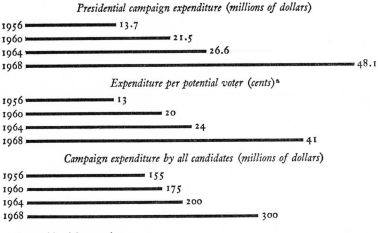

Presidential campaign expenditure (millions of dollars)

1956 ▬▬▬▬▬▬▬ 13.7
1960 ▬▬▬▬▬▬▬▬▬ 21.5
1964 ▬▬▬▬▬▬▬▬▬▬ 26.6
1968 ▬▬▬▬▬▬▬▬▬▬▬▬▬▬▬▬▬ 48.1

Expenditure per potential voter (cents)[a]

1956 ▬▬▬▬▬ 13
1960 ▬▬▬▬▬▬ 20
1964 ▬▬▬▬▬▬▬ 24
1968 ▬▬▬▬▬▬▬▬▬▬▬▬ 41

Campaign expenditure by all candidates (millions of dollars)

1956 ▬▬▬▬▬▬▬ 155
1960 ▬▬▬▬▬▬▬▬ 175
1964 ▬▬▬▬▬▬▬▬▬ 200
1968 ▬▬▬▬▬▬▬▬▬▬▬▬▬ 300

a. In presidential campaign.

1968 if spending for the Wallace campaign had not been included)
or the number of voters that candidates must reach.

Spending by all candidates campaigning for elective office increased much less rapidly than presidential campaign spending.
Presidential candidates were the first to adapt modern techniques
to their campaigns. They have employed a more diverse array of
methods than have many of the candidates for lesser offices, which
has driven their cost up faster. But high-cost technology, which
all candidates have increasingly used, prompted a great surge in
campaign costs at all levels of government between 1956 and 1968.

Growth in Broadcast Costs

Broadcast costs, the single largest item in most statewide and
national campaign budgets, have grown even faster than total costs.
Presidential and vice presidential candidates spent almost four
times as much for television in 1968 as they did in 1956, and their
expenditures for radio more than quintupled over the same period
(see Table 1). Presidential candidate spending for broadcasting

grew at a rate similar to that of all candidates, as a comparison of
Tables 1 and 2 indicates. Candidates generally expanded their
expenditures for radio at even faster rates than for television, although the latter still absorbs a larger amount of money.

Candidates' increased use of television accounts for only part
of the growing amounts they spend for it. Television stations and
networks generally charge more for their services now than they
did in 1956, as noted in Table 3, which shows the costs of dupli-
cating an advertising campaign in successive election years. Television spot advertising rates more than doubled between 1956 and

TABLE 3. Indicators of Long-Term Trends in Advertising
Costs

Advertising media	1956	1960	1964	1968
Business publications	100	126	150	189
Consumer magazines	100	137	158	180
Daily newspapers	100	116	132	149
Radio spots	100	106	121	143
Television spots	100	148	188	247

Source: *Media/scope,* December issues, 1960, p. 118; 1964, p. 114; 1968, p. 70. Published
as cost indexes by *Media/scope;* based on October prices each year.

1968, leading all competing media. The cost indicators do not
account for increased "circulation" of audience. Though the potential television audience probably grew much faster during this
period than those of competing media, the increase in cost of television spot time is nevertheless substantial. Network charges for
evening television program time varied only slightly, by comparison with those for spot advertising, as the following indicators of
cost changes (based on 1956) show:[11]

	1956	1960	1964	1968
Television programs	100	125	130	105

Voluntary reductions in charges in 1968 enabled candidates to buy
network program time then almost as cheaply as in 1956.

11. Computed from costs for thirty minutes of evening program time; cost figures
supplied by American Broadcasting Companies (ABC), Columbia Broadcasting System (CBS), and National Broadcasting Company (NBC).

These indicators of cost changes make it possible to compute what part of campaign cost increases between 1956 and 1968 resulted from increased charges for television time and what part represented an increase in the use of television:[12]

	Presidential candidates	Other candidates
Television expenditures, 1956	$3,669,897	$3,015,812
Increased time cost, 1968	2,378,660	4,433,244
Television expenditures, 1968	14,637,750	12,449,277
Increased use cost, 1968	8,589,193	5,000,221

Over three-fourths of presidential candidates' increased charges were due to increased use of television while those of all other candidates were only slightly greater for increased use than for increased charges.

EMPHASIS OF SPOTS

Since 1956, candidates have increasingly preferred spots to longer, program-length presentations, as is evident in Table 1. Whereas 85 percent of the presidential campaign expenditures for television network time was for programs in 1956, by 1968 only 52 percent went for programs and spots had risen from 15 to 48 percent of the costs. Figure 2 shows the trend of spot and program costs on both networks and local stations for all candidates in the 1956–68 period.

A major reason for the pronounced move to spot announcements is the larger audience they command. A veteran media expert explained: "It's very difficult to get people interested for more than

12. Increased time costs indicate the amount of additional money that would have been required in 1968 to duplicate the same time used in 1956. For presidential candidates this was figured by applying the 1968 advertising cost indicator for television spots to expenditures by these candidates in 1956 for spots on networks and to all expenditures on stations (which were more likely to be for spots than for program time). In addition, the 1968 indicator for network program time cost changes was applied to 1956 expenditures for network program time by presidential candidates. The procedure for computing increased time costs for other candidates was similar; however, the advertising cost indicator for 1968 was applied to all television expenditures by these candidates in 1956 since they were unlikely to use television network program time.

FIGURE 2. Percentages of General Election Television
Expenditures for Spot and Program Time on Networks and
Stations, 1956–68

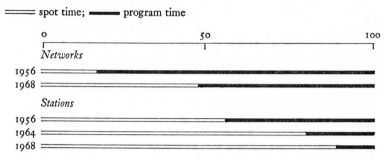

short periods of time. If you go longer than a minute it has to be *very* good." Another commented: "Spots are the only way you can get a lot of people. If you can get a minute in the Super Bowl, for example, you have something. A tremendous audience. It's usually impossible to get such an audience for a purely political program." More Americans prefer to watch an entertaining program or sports event than a political program of equivalent length, as Nielsen audience surveys readily demonstrate. In the fall of 1968, presidential campaign programs rarely attracted audiences that were more than half as large as those of several popular entertainment programs on which candidates could buy spots (see Figure 3). These political presentations attracted audiences about one-half to three-fourths the size of those of most shows they displaced; the greater the popularity of the preempted show, the greater the drop-off for the political program. Regular programs running at the same time as these political appearances drew larger audiences than they expected against their usual competitors, which indicates that viewers switch channels rather than turning their sets off. Presidential candidate political programs thus rarely attract large audiences. Few besides convinced partisans watch such shows. And if presidential candidates cannot attract large audiences for thirty-minute programs, it is doubtful that candidates for lesser offices can do any better.

Spot commercials reach larger audiences. Few viewers switch stations during a brief announcement. Uncommitted voters, or even those leaning toward his opponent, may hear the candidate's message. The candidate must often reach both to produce victory. For these reasons candidates pay the relatively high charges for short commercials, which cost almost as much as a full thirty minutes of program time. (The charge for thirty minutes of evening program time averaged $70,620 in 1968;[13] the cost of one minute of commercial time in October 1968 for programs like "Walt Disney," "Bonanza," "FBI," and "Jackie Gleason" ranged from $57,500 to $60,000.[14])

Candidates also prefer spots because of their flexibility. Increasingly, in sophisticated demographic profiles, program audiences are identified by viewers' age, sex, income, education, region of residence (and size of region), and even family size. A candidate can then focus his messages where he believes they will be most interesting, appealing, or pertinent. He may, for example, beam messages about social security or Medicare on programs viewed by large numbers of older citizens. Or he may choose programs that attract women to indicate his concern for peace. An office seeker might also heighten the impact of his message by transmitting it on a program with a complementary motif: he might stress law and order on a commercial shown on the program "FBI," for example; or he could communicate his opposition to gun control on a sports program. Spots, moreover, enable a candidate to develop a number of themes that he can use as events demand or in a planned frequency to "hit" given audiences.

Many stations prefer spots to program time and encourage candidates to use them. One media adviser complained: "We have trouble getting stations to make longer program time available. They prefer to sell one-minute, or less, spot time. This is the choice in everything but presidential races when the networks will sometimes make longer slots available." Broadcasters promote

13. Estimated from cost figures supplied by ABC, CBS, and NBC.
14. *NTI Cost per 1000 Commercial Minutes Report*, October 1968.

FIGURE 3. Size of Audiences of Thirty-Minute Programs of Presigrams with Spot Time Available, 1968

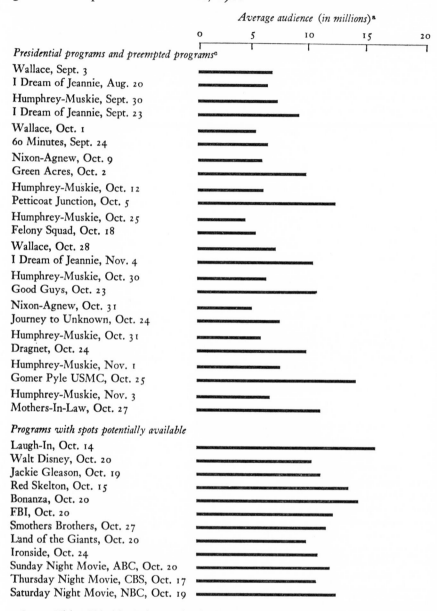

Source: Nielsen Television Index "National Nielsen TV Ratings" reports, Copyright, 1968, by A. C. Nielsen Company. Used by permission. The data are estimates only, subject to the definitions and reminders contained in the reports. The use of mathematical terms by Nielsen should not be regarded as a representation by Nielsen that such terms are exact to precise mathematical values.

a. Estimated number of television households tuned to a program during the average minute.

Share of total audience (percent)[b]   *Percent of preempted program audience*

Reported as percent of U.S. television households and as projected number of households reached, rounded to nearest 10,000 households.

b. Estimated audience during the average minute of a program. Reported as percent of households using television at the time of the program's principal telecast in the Eastern, Central, and Pacific Time Zones (Mountain Time Zone households included with Pacific or Central Time Zone).

c. Audience ratings of preempted programs are those for the most recent prior program.

spots partly because political programs lose audiences, and licensees fear that viewers lost to competing stations or networks on a given evening may not switch back. As audience sizes for successive programs go down, their attractiveness to advertisers decreases. Stations further fear that low ratings on a given evening might diminish advertising revenue for several weeks because ratings affect the price of time. Candidates' appearances on spots, however, will not lose the coveted audience to competitors.

Stations also prefer spots because they usually have several available on a given evening which they can use to accommodate several candidates. By contrast, the limited number of thirty-minute slots open in a given evening might not match the number of candidates wanting to use television. Networks, finally, may favor spots because ordinarily they earn more from selling several commercial minutes during a thirty-minute program than from selling the entire thirty minutes to a candidate at program-time rates.

EMPHASIS OF STATIONS

Candidates buy television broadcast time either on networks (which then share the revenue with their affiliates in accordance with complex formulas) or on local stations. Between 1956 and 1968 their spending for station time increased much more rapidly than for network time (see Tables 1 and 2). The percentages of television budgets devoted to stations (see Figure 4) have grown as the number of candidates below the presidency using television has grown. Presidential candidates pioneered in the use of television, concentrating their efforts on networks. Local candidates, who could not use network television economically, followed later by buying time on local stations that covered their districts.

Even presidential candidates have increasingly preferred stations over networks since 1956. This is a direct result of technological advance: Polls and computer analysis pinpoint areas needing special emphasis to create a winning coalition and identify issues particularly appealing to persons living there. Advertising

FIGURE 4. Percentages of Television Expenditures Made to Networks and Stations, General Elections, 1956–68

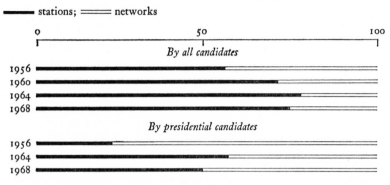

agencies and media buyers purchase local station time all over the nation. Presidential candidates, holding time on stations located in areas they want to emphasize, beam messages especially designed to appeal to local residents, thus relating their campaigns to issues of local interest (or controversy).[15] Station buying also allows national candidates to emphasize different mixtures of issues in different places; presidential candidates can thus concentrate their efforts where they count most, without wasting money either in hopeless areas or in areas they will carry with little effort.

Frequently presidential candidates can obtain more favorable cancellation and discount policies on local stations than on networks. These help the candidate place his commercial where he wants it at an advantageous price. Spending on local stations also provides a form of local patronage. Broadcasters are often influential locally (many, for example, also own local newspapers). Although large spending does not "buy" local station owners and personnel, it does not usually make enemies either.

PRODUCTION COSTS

The broadcast expenses thus far discussed include only time charges. Production costs—charges for preparing a candidate's

15. For a discussion of Richard Nixon's use of this device, see Joe McGinnis, *The Selling of the President 1968* (Trident, 1969), especially pp. 11–25, 120–25.

program or commercial—should also be included to reflect the true expenses of broadcast time. For example, the production cost of a thirty-minute television documentary ranged from $50,000 to $200,000 in 1968, and for a package of ten spots from $25,000 to $75,000.[16] If a candidate uses many different programs and spots, production costs can be a major expense item. But candidate expenditure reports do not usually provide these figures. The political broadcasting surveys of the Federal Communications Commission, moreover, do not include production charges, which candidates usually pay to consultants or film companies rather than to stations. It is thus impossible to accurately ascertain these charges. From the sporadic reports available, Herbert E. Alexander estimates that total production costs for national campaigns range from one-fifth to one-third as much as time charges.[17]

Inadequate reporting makes it impossible to compare production costs over several election years. Between 1956 and 1968, however, candidates increasingly turned to high-cost film makers and producers to create products that would attract audiences and communicate effectively. It is thus probable that production costs have increased at least as fast as time costs. Since modern-day political programing contains less and less of the low-cost walk-on-speech routines that were once prevalent, production costs may have increased even faster than time costs.

Comparison of Growth in Television and Campaign Costs

Although office seekers' total campaign costs have increased markedly since 1956, their broadcasting costs have increased at even faster rates (see Tables 1 and 2). Assuming that available figures accurately reflect the growth rate of these costs (even if they do not measure all campaign and television expenses), broadcast expenses consumed a larger and larger share of campaign

16. Costs estimated by Public Affairs Analysts, Washington.
17. *Campaign Broadcast Reform Act of 1969*, Hearings, p. 177.

budgets between 1956 and 1968. In Figure 5 these increases are compared with increases in the gross national product, the consumer price index, the cost of spot television time, the estimated population of voting age, and the number of homes with television. The growth rates of these factors, all measured from a common point, indicate that total campaign spending at the national level and television costs grew at dramatically greater rates than most of the other items. Comparatively, the 30 percent growth in the consumer price index during the twelve-year period appears very modest. And the voting population—which candidates spend their money to reach—grew by only 15 percent. These comparisons, perhaps more than any other, emphasize the magnitude of increased costs of campaigning for public office in this country.

Conclusions

Candidates increasingly use television because they believe it is the only way, or at least the most effective way, to reach voters. The ubiquity of the television set and its ability to attract audiences, and in consequence the great potential impact of the electronic message, account for television's strength. Comparing television commercials with newspaper ads, a media adviser to a recent presidential candidate commented: "The impact of a television commercial is likely to be more dramatic on those who see it. You have the voice, the color (in about 40 percent of the homes), the music. All of this permits you to make much more of an impact." Sight, sound, and color combine as formidable weapons in the struggle to reach voters with campaign messages.

Candidates emphasize television because they believe it works. Their calculations are not necessarily the refined products of careful research and long cogitation. Campaigning is an imitative art, and impressions frequently communicate information that becomes rules to candidates and campaign managers. In recent years, campaigns emphasizing television have, at times, been very visibly and spectacularly successful. Milton Shapp, a virtual un-

FIGURE 5. Indicators of Campaign Costs Compared with
Other National Indicators, 1956–68

1956 = 100

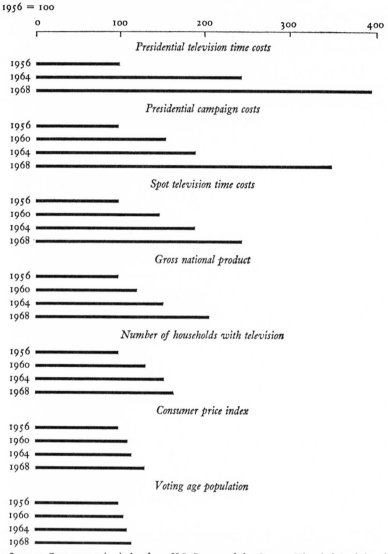

Sources: Consumer price index from U.S. Bureau of the Census, *Historical Statistics of the United States, Continuation to 1962 and Revisions,* p. 19, and *Statistical Abstract of the United States, 1969,* p. 345; gross national product from *Statistical Abstract ... 1969,* p. 311, and *Historical Statistics of the United States, Colonial Times to 1957,* p. 139; number of households with television from *Nielsen TV 1969* (New York: A. C. Nielsen Co.); population of voting age from *Statistical Abstract ... 1969,* p. 368; spot television time costs from Table 3; presidential campaign costs and presidential television time costs from Table 1.

known, used huge television expenditures to beat the hand-picked gubernatorial candidate of the theretofore formidable Pennsylvania Democratic party (in 1966). Governor Nelson Rockefeller (in 1966) and Mayor John Lindsay (in 1969) blanketed their constituencies with television to stave off what looked to many like certain defeats. Mike Gravel (in 1968) won a Democratic nomination for senator in Alaska over an entrenched official who had been a historic figure in Alaskan development. And Howard Metzenbaum, a relatively unknown lawyer and businessman, defeated America's first astronaut, John Glenn, in a 1970 primary for a U.S. Senate nomination. This impressive list of victories through television establishes it as the campaign medium of the time. Those who need to use it and who have the skill to exploit it find that deploying it effectively requires large expenditures. This is why television costs have driven up campaign expenditures over the last twelve years.

These soaring campaign costs impose immense burdens on candidates for public office. The large sums must be raised in relatively short periods of time. As the burdens of fund raising become greater and more visible, they stimulate the search for a new policy that promises relief.

Chapter Three

☆

APPROACHES AND REACTIONS TO REFORM

DEMANDS for reform generated important legislative activity in 1970 and 1971. Of the numerous proposals advanced in Congress, several contained provisions similar to those of the 1970 campaign finance reform bill.[1] This bill passed both houses of Congress but was vetoed by President Richard Nixon.

The 1970 Campaign Finance Reform Bill

The proposed legislation would have suspended, for presidential and vice presidential candidates, the equal time requirements imposed by Section 315(a) of the Communications Act, which states:

> If any licensee shall permit any person who is a legally qualified candidate for any public office to use a broadcasting station, he shall afford equal opportunities to all other such candidates for that office in the use of such broadcasting station: Provided, That such licensee shall have no power of censorship over the material broadcast under the provisions of this section. No obligation is hereby imposed upon any licensee to allow the use of its station by any such candidate.

Whether a station provides its facilities free of charge or for a price, it must upon providing time to one candidate provide it on

---

1. For detailed provisions of the bill, see *Congressional Record* (daily ed.), Nov. 23, 1970, pp. S18723–S18724.

equal terms to all other contestants for the same office. But the requirement does not extend to candidates for other offices, even those running in the same election. It is the station's prerogative to choose whether or not to sell or give time to the candidates for any office in the first place.

Broadcasters often contend that the equal time requirement can restrict the amount of free time that stations offer, particularly to candidates for the presidency.[2] They might willingly provide free time to major presidential candidates, for example, but be loathe to do so for the less significant. Section 315(a), however, requires that equal time be extended to every candidate contesting for the same office. Broadcasters consequently tend to offer no time at all. Had the 1970 finance reform bill been signed into law, stations could have granted free time to the two or three major presidential candidates without having to do the same for the dozen or so others.

Modification or suspension of Section 315 of the Communications Act is the most popular of the many proposals to reform campaign financing. Between 1955 and 1970, members of Congress introduced over thirty bills aimed at excluding from the equal time requirements candidates ranging from presidential only to all those running for public office.

The 1970 reform bill provided benefits to all office seekers by requiring stations to sell time at reduced cost. It would have compelled broadcasting licensees (including cable television facilities) to sell time to all legally qualified candidates at a price "not [to] exceed the lowest unit charge of the station for the same amount of time in the same time period."[3] Charges vary for the same spot of time primarily because of the limitations of the broadcast day. By contrast with the printed media, the broadcast media cannot expand and contract the amount of time available for commercial exploitation in accordance with demand. The price for a given

2. *Political Broadcasting—1970*, Hearings before the House Committee on Interstate and Foreign Commerce, 91 Cong. 2 sess. (1970), pp. 67–68, 74–75, 88.
3. *Congressional Record* (daily ed.), Nov. 23, 1970, p. S18723.

spot of time is thus very closely tied to advertisers' demand for it. Highly rated evening shows usually attract the highest prices from advertisers because of the large audience they reach. Less popular programs sell for less because they reach fewer people.

Broadcasters also try to assure that the time slots for commercials will be filled on their programs. They accordingly grant discounts to encourage advertisers to buy large numbers of spots and they expand the discounts if the commercials can be used in unsold time positions. Time is often sold at less than the going rate simply because it has not been filled. A network executive explained: "If A&P has a batch of bananas on Saturday and they aren't moving, they will lower the prices to get them out of the store. They will be stale on Monday. The same thing is true for broadcasters. If you have holes to fill on a ballgame, you get the rate down to try to get them filled, even if the price was higher two weeks before. You don't want to get into the program with unfilled time because it is lost if you do." Broadcasters' practices and advertisers' demands combine to produce considerable variation in the price of a one-minute commercial spot during a given evening. Political candidates seldom qualify for the highest discounts because their demands are short term.

Section 315(b) of the Communications Act requires that charges to candidates "shall not exceed the charges made for comparable use of such station for other purposes." Stations thus cannot charge candidates any more than they charge any advertiser for a similar time slot. This does prevent stations from following the practice of many newspapers, which charge candidates premium rates for advertising. The 1970 reform bill would have gone an extra step, compelling stations to charge political advertisers the cheapest rate for a given time segment—and that can be considerably less than the highest rate they charge.

Another feature of the 1970 reform proposal limited the amount that candidates for the offices of president (and vice president), U.S. senator and representative, governor and lieutenant governor of a state could spend for the use of broadcasting time. For the general election the bill limited broadcast spending by each office seeker to seven cents times the number of votes cast for all candidates for the contested office in the last election, or $20,000, whichever was greater. For primary elections each candidate (excepting the presidential candidates) was limited to one-half the general election limit. To enforce these spending ceilings the bill required each candidate, or his authorized representative, to certify in writing to a station that his buying of a requested amount of time would not violate the limits. Stations could not sell time to candidates unwilling to sign such an affidavit.

The reform proposal's principal authors feared that without limitations on spending, rate reductions would do little to reduce total campaign costs. Candidates could spend customary amounts for broadcasting and reap the advantage of getting more time for the same amount of money. Spending ceilings, by contrast, could decrease total campaign costs.

THE PRESIDENTIAL VETO

Like most individuals, President Richard Nixon does not oppose reform. But he did object to the particular path outlined by the 1970 political broadcast reform proposal, which he described in his veto message as having a "good aim, gone amiss."[4] Chief among the President's objections was his belief that the bill was not comprehensive enough: "The problem with campaign spending is not radio and television; the problem is spending. This bill plugs only one hole in a sieve."[5] Presumably the President disagrees with the contention of the bill's sponsors that a first step toward reform is a beneficial advance. The President also felt that the bill discriminated against broadcasters. Because the ceilings applied only to broadcast expenditures, radio and television were placed at a competitive disadvantage. And since candidates could divert their spending to other items, the President believed that overall campaign spending might remain unaffected. The proposal compounds

4. *Ibid.*, Oct. 12, 1970, p. S17801.
5. *Ibid.*

the discrimination against the broadcasting industry by singling it out for mandatory rate reductions for political advertising. The President charged that such reductions comprised government rate setting. In addition, President Nixon feared that the proposal, by imposing ceilings on broadcast expenditures, would make it difficult for office seekers—particularly those wishing to challenge incumbents—to get their message to voters. Normally, incumbents attract attention during their tenure and are better known than their opponents by the time of the election. To overcome this advantage, challengers frequently need to outspend them during the campaign in order to establish identity among voters. Since the bill proposed equal limits on incumbent and challenger, the President feared it would preserve the incumbent's advantages. The President objected to the bill on a number of administrative grounds as well, contending that it would be difficult to enforce and that the limitation formula was based on "political compromise" rather than on scientific calculations of broadcast markets and costs. For all of these reasons he sent the bill back to Congress with his veto.

CONGRESSIONAL REACTION TO THE VETO

In January 1972 Congress belatedly enacted a reform bill known as the Federal Election Campaign Act of 1971. It raised the spending limits imposed by the 1970 bill from seven cents per voter to ten cents and based the limitation on estimated voting age population rather than the more cumbersome number of votes cast in the previous election. Limitations on spending were extended to newspapers, magazines, billboard advertising, and mass telephone canvasses, with no more than 60 percent of a candidate's funds to be spent on broadcasting. The "lowest rate charged" discount was retained for broadcasting advertising, while newspapers and magazines were allowed to charge political advertisers no more than the rate charged commercial advertisers, thus eliminating premium rates for candidate advertising. These limitations and provisions sought to meet the President's objections to the 1970 bill.

The 1971 bill also tightened the disclosure features of existing laws and limited the amount a candidate or his immediate family might contribute to his own campaign. The Senate version of the bill had extended the repeal of Section 315(a) to all candidates for federal office; because of opposition both in the House of Representatives and in the White House, the final version of the bill did not even include repeal of Section 315(a) for presidential and vice presidential candidates.[6]

Whatever the hopes of the bill's sponsors, the likelihood is great that most of the problems of financing outlined earlier in this study will not be resolved. Moreover, the legislation is subject to the broad questions of application discussed later in the study.

Additional Policy Options

The principal components of the 1970 and 1971 reform proposals—advertising rate discounts, permanent suspension (in the 1970 bill) of Section 315(a) of the Communications Act, and spending ceilings for advertising—applied to particular groups of candidates and specific elections. Future proposals will likely choose from among a number of components that include these plus other possibilities. Many of the possible additional components have been a part of proposals advanced in the past.

FREE SERVICES

To counter the difficulties of campaign financing, a number of plans have introduced a component of free service. These proposals generally advocate free broadcast time, postal services, or voter registration. The Twentieth Century Fund recently advanced "Voters' Time," which would provide from two to six hours of prime television time to presidential candidates, depending on the strength of their parties in past elections.[7] Programs—offered "substantially live" to assure the highest possible educational

6. See *Congressional Record* (daily ed.), Dec. 14, 1971, pp. H12467–H12476, for provisions of this bill.

7. See Twentieth Century Fund, *Voters' Time* (New York: Twentieth Century Fund, 1969). Bills incorporating provisions similar to this plan include S. 1, introduced on Jan. 25, 1971, by Senator Gravel and others, and H.R. 5090, introduced by Representative Anderson and others on Feb. 25, 1971.

quality—would be beamed at the same time in each time zone by all broadcast facilities. Cost for the time would be split between government and broadcasters, with the Treasury paying for the time and broadcasters charging for the time at a 50 percent discount, or the lowest charge made to any commercial advertiser for such time, whichever is lower.

Several proponents of "free television time" for candidates have settled the cost entirely on broadcasters. Former President Dwight Eisenhower alluded to their proposals: "It has . . . been suggested that the radio and television industry should give a reasonable amount of free prime time to candidates for important offices during major campaigns. After all, the air waves belong to the people and are only licensed to the stations; it would not be unreasonable to insist that in return the networks contribute this public service."[8] But during his tenure, Eisenhower never proposed this in legislative form. Another advocate, the United Auto Workers, has recommended making "mandatory and broadening the free TV and radio time so successfully accorded the political parties in the [1960] campaign."[9] Senator Hubert Humphrey in 1956 and Senators Warren Magnuson and Mike Monroney in 1960 introduced bills requiring television networks to provide up to one hour each week to each eligible presidential candidate.[10]

A second major service advanced in several finance reform proposals (including a bill introduced by Representative John B. Anderson in 1970 and again in 1971[11]) centers on providing postal services to candidates or party organizations. One possible postal service would provide candidates one or two free mailings. An-

8. Dwight D. Eisenhower, "The Ticklish Problem of Political Fund Raising and Spending," *Reader's Digest*, Vol. 92 (January 1968), p. 68.

9. See *Congressional Record*, Vol. 113, Pt. 15, 90 Cong. 1 sess. (1967), p. 20364.

10. See *Digest of General Public Bills*, prepared by the Legislative Reference Service of the Library of Congress, 84 Cong. 2 sess. (1956), p. S3962; and *Congressional Quarterly Almanac* (Washington: Congressional Quarterly Service, 1960), Vol. 16, pp. 290–91.

11. H.R. 19904 introduced on Dec. 2, 1970, and H.R. 5093 introduced on Feb. 25, 1971. Other plans containing a postal service component include Committee for Economic Development, *Financing A Better Election System* (New York: CED, 1968), pp. 22, 44; and Twentieth Century Fund, *Electing Congress* (Twentieth Century Fund, 1970), pp. 23–24.

other would permit candidates or party organizations to use the lowest rate available to charitable organizations—a lower rate than that presently available to them.

The voter registration effort of candidates and party organizations often requires major expenditures. The Committee for Economic Development proposes to lighten that burden by easing restrictive voter registration laws, which, implicitly, would reduce the cost of registering voters.[12] Other plans propose that the states or federal government assume the burden and cost of canvassing election districts and keeping up-to-date lists of eligible voters.[13]

In 1971 over a dozen bills dealing with voting registration were introduced in Congress. Several proposed a more direct responsibility for the federal government in registering voters (S. 2574, providing for registration by mail, received committee approval but died on the Senate floor).

VOLUNTARY RATE DISCOUNTS

Another approach to alleviating the difficulties of campaign financing consists of voluntary rate discounts by broadcasting stations, which might reduce campaign advertising costs. Stations could offer candidates the same discounts they provide to volume advertisers (a voluntary version of the required rate discount provision in the 1970 reform bill); the charge to candidates for advertising time would not exceed the lowest charge to volume advertisers for the same time. Or the candidate could be charged the maximum rate for a given time period and given a straight discount. Approximately 40 of the 680 operating commercial television stations in the United States have already offered voluntary discounts to candidates.[14] The straight discounts have ranged from 25 to 50 percent.

12. *Financing a Better Election System*, pp. 22, 31–33.

13. Democratic National Committee, *That All May Vote* (Washington: Democratic National Committee, 1969), especially pp. 7–9.

14. Federal Communications Commission (FCC), *35th Annual Report/Fiscal Year 1969*, p. 125, indicates there are 680 stations operating in the United States. For reductions offered, see *Congressional Record* (daily ed.), Oct. 14, 1970, p. E9373; and *The Campaign Broadcast Reform Act of 1969*, Hearings before the Senate Committee on Commerce, 91 Cong. 1 sess. (1969), pp. 53, 62, 111, 119, 125, 165, 167, 180.

TAX INCENTIVES

Tax incentives are designed to encourage citizens to contribute more liberally to candidates and political parties. The Revenue Act of 1971, passed by Congress and signed by the President in December, contains tax incentives for campaign contributions. The taxpayer may opt for a tax credit or deduction on campaign contributions up to $50 for a single taxpayer and $100 for married taxpayers filing jointly. The tax credit reduces the tax bill by one-half of the amount of the contribution; the deduction reduces taxable income by the full amount of the contribution. The credit or deduction may apply to contributions to any candidate for public office in any election.[15] Of all the legislative changes made during 1971, this provision is the most likely to produce more money for the 1972 political campaigns.

MONEY

Providing money to candidates directly from the public treasury is another possible reform. The Presidential Election Campaign Fund Act of 1966 permitted each taxpayer to contribute $1 of his federal taxes to such a fund by checking the appropriate box on his tax return. From this fund the federal treasury would pay equal amounts to each political party whose presidential candidate had received at least fifteen million votes in the preceding election. Since about sixty million votes are cast in most presidential elections, and since two parties usually receive most of the votes, in a normal year the national Republican and Democratic treasuries would be entitled to approximately $30 million each under the bill, provided a large enough group of taxpayers had checked the contribution box on their tax returns. The law guaranteed a fund of at least $5 million. The act also designated that any minor party

15. For an explanation, see the House-Senate conference committee report in *Congressional Record* (daily ed.), Dec. 4, 1971, pp. S20611–S20612. For other tax incentive proposals, see Twentieth Century Fund, *Electing Congress*, pp. 22–23; CED, *Financing a Better Election System*, pp. 21, 49–51; *Political Campaign Financing Proposals*, Hearings before the Senate Committee on Finance, 90 Cong. 1 sess. (1967), pp. 10–11, 18, 25–26, 49, 50–51.

(whose candidate in the preceding election had received between five and fifteen million votes) would receive $1 for every vote in excess of five million that its candidate had received in the previous election.[16] This law, the first massive federal effort to finance campaigns, was made inoperative by Congress in 1967, before it took effect.

Another direct money proposal, advanced by Senator Albert Gore of Tennessee, provided candidates for federal office the option of relying on public or private financing of their campaigns. Major party candidates (whose predecessors had received at least 20 percent of the popular vote in the last election) opting for public funding would receive from the federal treasury an amount equal to twenty cents times the number of votes cast for the office in the previous election. Minor party candidates (whose predecessors had received between 5 and 20 percent of the popular vote) choosing public funding would receive forty cents multiplied by the number of votes cast in the current election, provided that they received at least 5 percent of the total. The main features of the Gore plan were incorporated by the Senate Finance Committee in the 1967 honest elections proposal, a bill that was not enacted. That proposal defined minor party candidates as those receiving between 5 and 25 (rather than 20) percent of the vote in the previous election and limited federal financing to candidates for president, vice president, and senator (rather than covering candidates for the House of Representatives as well).[17]

A third plan, introduced by Senator Lee Metcalf of Montana, proposed a voucher system to allocate federal money to candidates. This plan permits the U.S. Treasury to return a voucher worth $1 to taxpayers. The taxpayer then gives the certificate to the candidate (or party organization) of his choice, who then redeems it for cash at the federal treasury.[18]

16. For provisions of this law, see *Political Campaign Financing Proposals*, Hearings, pp. 63–65.

17. *Ibid.*, pp. 44–50.

18. *Ibid.*, pp. 11–14. A proposal introduced by Senators Gravel and Randolph as S. 9 on Jan. 25, 1971, would provide money directly to presidential and congressional

A new tax checkoff plan, similar to that in the 1966 act, became law with the passage of the Revenue Act of 1971. The new plan funnels money directly to the presidential nominee of the party rather than to the national committee, in part to quiet fears that such committees might use the funds prior to nominating conventions to influence the choice there. The new plan also permits the nominee to choose between public and private financing, as proposed in the Gore bill. The money allotted major party nominees is based on fifteen cents per eligible voter (a maximum of approximately $20.4 million for each candidate in 1972). Nominees of minor parties (that received between 5 and 25 percent of the vote in the prior or current election) would receive one-fourth the amount received by major party nominees.[19] Under the 1971 plan, a taxpayer may designate the party nominee he wishes to allocate his $1 checkoff to, or specify that it go to a general fund to be used by minor party candidates or by major party nominees if allocated funds do not reach the maximum amounts permitted.

The new checkoff provision will not affect the 1972 presidential election since it is to take effect on January 1, 1973. Moreover, President Richard Nixon bitterly opposed the plan and promised to see that it was never implemented.[20] He could do so most easily by vetoing the appropriations legislation necessary to make the bill operative. There is thus no guarantee that this far-reaching legislation will ever be implemented.

REGULATING CONTRIBUTIONS AND EXPENDITURES

Campaign finance laws have consisted chiefly of limits, prohibitions, and disclosures. Federal laws have limited what candidates

---

candidates. It authorizes subsidies for election expenses up to an amount based on the basic formula of twenty cents per vote received by the party's candidate in the previous election. Parties fielding candidates who received at least 10 percent of the vote in the previous election are eligible for funds.

19. For an explanation of the tax checkoff provisions of the Revenue Act of 1971 see *Congressional Record* (daily ed.), Dec. 4, 1971, pp. S20611–S20612.

20. See the statement by Press Secretary Ronald L. Ziegler, *New York Times*, Dec. 3, 1971.

could spend and contributors could give. They have prohibited donations from banks, corporations, and labor unions, and they have outlawed the soliciting of federal employees for campaign gifts. These laws also have required public disclosure of the names of contributors who gave above a certain amount and have required candidates to report expenditures. Many current proposals, like the ceiling on advertising expenditures and the disclosure requirements contained in the 1971 election reform law, are offered as improvements of these restraints.

Two reform groups, the Twentieth Century Fund and the Committee for Economic Development, have recently advanced proposals containing prohibition and disclosure components.[21] Both recommended repealing limits on the size of contributions and on total campaign expenditures. In place of this they would emphasize reporting and publication of gifts and expenditures. Each would require committees supporting candidates to report receipts and expenditures as well as compel contributors giving large amounts (an aggregate of $5,000 is proposed by the Twentieth Century Fund and of $500 by the CED) to make independent reports of these to a federal elections committee. Both also recommend more stringent laws requiring national registration of committees supporting political candidates. Contributors would also have to certify that they were not being reimbursed for their contributions; this requirement is designed to thwart any attempt of businesses, banks, and labor unions (who may not make contributions directly) to use individuals as conduits for their political contributions. Recent bills introduced by Senator James Pearson of Kansas and Representative John Anderson of Illinois incorporate similar provisions.[22] The latter proposal also includes limitations on total expenditures by candidates contesting for federal offices.

21. See Twentieth Century Fund, *Electing Congress*, pp. 15–21; and CED, *Financing a Better Election System*, pp. 21–22, 25, 53–65.

22. S. 1692, introduced March 26, 1969, and H.R. 19904, introduced Dec. 2, 1970. For other such bills, see *Political Campaign Financing Proposals*, Hearings, pp. 27–33, 34–44, 50–52. See also H.R. 5087, introduced by Representative Anderson and others on Feb. 25, 1971

Reactions to Reform

A number of groups are likely to have strong reactions to any proposal for campaign finance reform. Among the most visible are elected public officials, present contributors, political parties, political consultants, broadcasters, the Federal Communications Commission, and various reform groups.

ELECTED PUBLIC OFFICIALS

Campaign financing vitally affects elected public officials since they must regularly mount campaigns in the struggle to continue in office. As legal decision makers they also determine government policy in this area.

Because campaign financing affects elected officials' life-blood—how they get elected and the type of opposition they face—most of them do not remain disinterested or dispassionate. Achieving high elective office does not usually come easily. It often requires mastery of an intricate process of recruitment, filling of a succession of offices without serious mistakes, and a measure of good luck.

Incumbents possess many advantages that decrease their costs of campaigning. Officeholders can produce the favors that some contributors seek; this reduces many incumbents' task of raising money. Frequently, officeholders have access to contributors outside their constituencies; the favors they grant while holding office can often be repaid with cash contributions at campaign time. Adroit givers, moreover, seek to help winners (since they can deliver favors), and incumbents usually stand a better chance of winning. No wonder a congressional aide observed, "An incumbent figures that no matter how high the costs he's usually in a better situation to raise more money than a potential challenger."

For these reasons, elected officials generally base their judgment of any campaign finance proposal on their calculation of how it will affect their advantages. Since incumbents usually have better access to money and services than do challengers, they usually conclude that plans providing these "will help potential opponents even more," as one staffer put it. Officials, however, may react positively to finance changes that limit expenditures, particularly during primary campaigns. They may view this as protection against possible challenges by rich opponents (often with no prior political experience) who could easily outspend them. Officials might also favor spending limitations for items like broadcasting (as in the 1970 and 1971 reform bills) because with their prior identification advantages, they may not have to spend as much as their challengers to establish their identity with the voting public. They could thus calculate that equal expenditures would be more disadvantageous to their opponents than to themselves.

PRESENT CONTRIBUTORS

Large contributors to political campaigns are presently rewarded with many advantages. As one official noted, they may be reluctant to relinquish those advantages: "Some [contributors] may bitch because they have to 'pony-up' $300,000 during a presidential campaign. But when they think about doing something [to bring reform] they stop. . . . They realize that the present way of doing things works to their advantage." For this reason, reforms designed to reduce candidates' dependence upon large contributors might not receive widespread support from present large givers.

POLITICAL PARTIES

National political party committees maintain an important stake in campaign financing, especially in presidential campaigns. They organize the fund-raising committees. They contract for campaign services. In the end they assume the campaign debt, if there is one. There usually is, for rarely does a presidential campaign finish without a modest debt. The staggering debt of more than $8 million that devolved to the Democratic National Committee is equally rare, but a proven possibility.

Party fund-raising performances. Over the years the Republicans have consistently raised more money for presidential campaigns than have the Democrats. They outspent the Democrats in twelve of the fifteen presidential campaigns since 1912.[23] The more conservative stance of the Republican party finds a friendly reception among those with big money, which facilitates the party's efforts to tap these sources. Moreover, voting behavior studies regularly find that more high-income persons identify with the Republican party than with the Democratic,[24] which provides the Republicans a somewhat more lucrative base to tap than the Democrats. Furthermore, high-income persons are also much more likely to participate in politics generally,[25] which means that they can be somewhat more easily induced to contribute than their lower income counterparts (who tend to identify with the Democrats). Thus the differences in the parties' bases of support make fund raising easier for Republicans.

The Republican party further expands its advantages by energetically pursuing the small contributor. While the Democrats were neglecting the "nickel and dime" giver in favor of the large donor during the 1960s, the Republicans increased their base of contributors, largely through direct mail soliciting. This produced a noticeable payoff. The sustaining membership of the Republican party finances its sizable nonelection year expenses (in excess of $2 million) while the Democrats until early 1971 went even deeper in debt to finance their more modest operations.[26]

Republicans rely primarily on large contributors, however, to finance presidential campaigns. According to one study: "In 1968, Republican fund drives produced $6,600,000 in gifts averaging almost $15 each from 450,000 individual contributors. But it was the Republican revival among large contributors, especially among

23. Congressional Quarterly Service, *Politics in America 1945–68*, 3rd ed. (Washington: Congressional Quarterly Service, May 1969), p. 114.

24. See Angus Campbell, Gerald Gurin, and Warren E. Miller, *The Voter Decides* (Row, Peterson, 1954), especially p. 73; Angus Campbell and others, *The American Voter* (Wiley, 1960), especially pp. 156–59; and Bernard Berelson, Paul F. Lazarsfeld, and William N. McPhee, *Voting* (University of Chicago Press, 1954), p. 56.

25. See Lester W. Milbrath, *Political Participation* (Rand McNally, 1965), pp. 120–21.

26. The Democratic National Committee's operating deficit for 1969, a nonelection year, was $400,000 (*Washington Post*, March 23, 1970).

businessmen, that really paid the G.O.P.'s way in 1968."[27] If a party successfully generating gifts from small contributors cannot rely on them to finance presidential campaigns, it is doubtful that small contributors offer a viable solution to campaign financing difficulties. A party official (Republican), for example, noted: "I don't agree that the parties could raise all of the money that they need if they were more energetic about it. Now I will say this. They can raise enough to sustain themselves—to meet their regular operating expenses. We are proving that you can do that. . . . But campaigns require so much money that it's impossible to put enough aside to run a campaign like it should be."

As for the Democrats, by 1968 they found themselves increasingly deserted by their large contributors who sought better fortunes elsewhere, generally by returning to the Republican party. This sharpened the Democrats' need to build a large base of small contributors. By 1970 the party appeared to have reversed its earlier policy of neglecting the pursuit of small contributors.

Republican advantages. Although several Republican members of Congress have supported reform, the Republican party generally responds coolly to campaign finance reform. President Richard Nixon, a Republican, vetoed the 1970 reform bill. During interviews for this study, no Republican party official or member of the 1968 Nixon campaign organization embraced finance reform. Democrats in comparable positions, by contrast, vigorously espoused a variety of plans. Republicans' evaluations of finance reform will likely rest on their desire to preserve their present edge in raising funds. According to one party official (Democrat) this concern fueled the Nixon administration's opposition to a tax incentive reform proposed during the 1969 tax legislation debate in the U.S. Senate. He explained: "They said it was a revenue loss decision. But it wouldn't have cost over $50 or $60 million at the most—which is peanuts. What really concerned them was that any bill would help the Democrats more than the Republicans. They aren't

27. Herbert Alexander and Harold B. Meyers, "A Financial Landslide for the G.O.P.," *Fortune*, March 1970, p. 104.

having any financial trouble now and rarely do. . . . So their pure political calculation was that this bill would help us [Democrats] more than it would them." Republicans also generally approach changes requiring more government regulation or expense with caution. These concerns combine to create resistance to campaign finance reform among Republican party officials.

Intraparty strife. Intraparty strife also plays a part in party responses to finance proposals. The Republican finance organization is much more centralized and united than that of the Democrats. A United Republican Finance Committee, for example, coordinates fund raising activities of the Republican National Committee, the Republican Senatorial Campaign Committee, and the Republican Congressional Campaign Committee. No counterpart exists for the Democrats. Democratic party officials appear much more sensitive to control of party money than do their Republican counterparts. They also seem much more wary of lodging control in the national committee.

This concern blocked operation of the Presidential Election Campaign Fund Act in the 1968 campaign. The Democratic Senatorial and Congressional Campaign Committees and some state committees feared that National Committee control of the distribution of these funds would increase the power of that committee at their expense. Widespread acrimony among Democrats, fanned by disputes over presidential handling of the Vietnam hostilities, augmented this fear. Many felt that President Lyndon Johnson would use the riches flowing to the Democratic National Committee to finance his own primary and general election campaign in 1968 and to reward friends and punish enemies in their election struggles.

Organizational prerogatives and ideological differences divide parties, which are already decentralized.[28] One of the powerful political resources within the parties falls to the factions or organizations that distribute money. For this reason public and party

28. For a discussion of party organization, see Frank J. Sorauf, *Political Parties in the American System* (Little, Brown, 1964), pp. 6–8.

officials carefully scrutinize the allocation devices provided by reform proposals.

Third party considerations. The growth of a viable third party in national politics could affect reactions to finance reform proposals. Many previously staunch supporters of change may hesitate to support campaign reforms that create financial benefits for the American Independent party (AIP). Yet a party polling nearly 15 percent of the popular vote cannot be ignored. Major parties, traditionally resistant to the entry of new parties into the electoral arena, may succumb to (or even use) that excuse for opposing reform. And AIP supporters or sympathizers may themselves impede reform. The party generally opposes extending federal power on grounds that onerous controls inevitably accompany new programs. One AIP activist commented, "I just don't want to see [the federal government's] power extended to this area." Moreover, some AIP sympathizers in Congress may join the ranks of reform opposition simply because they believe the benefits charted by various finance plans may not provide the American Independent party money or services commensurate with its strength. Proposals giving all benefits (or all but a small fraction) to the two major parties could generate such opposition. Other members of Congress, perhaps fighting to stave off third party threats to their own futures, may question the wisdom of providing AIP candidates a financial boost at just this time.

POLITICAL CONSULTANTS

Political consultants, whose role in modern campaigning is increasing, have an intense interest in campaign financing. Their services command high fees. The technology they manipulate requires huge outlays. Those who have served underfinanced campaigns know the limitations imposed on the candidate who cannot afford the massive technological support required by a modern campaign. One consultant related: "Not having money hurt us during the [1968] Humphrey campaign. We couldn't plan our media campaign as well because the broadcast people make you pay in advance. . . . It also cuts down on how much you're able to do." Consultants thus focus their evaluation of finance reform proposals on the campaign itself, where adequate money is crucial to their performing the services for which they are hired. It is not surprising that the consultants interviewed for this study and those who have testified at public hearings have more consistently than any other group advocated changes in campaign financing.[29] At one of their periodic study seminars in November of 1970 the American Association of Political Consultants passed a resolution urging Congress to override the President's veto of the 1970 campaign finance reform bill.[30]

The consultants' task in a campaign—devising the most appropriate technological and issue mix for candidates—predisposes them to support proposals that preserve the greatest possible flexibility for the candidate. The vicissitudes of any given campaign coupled with differences among candidates and election districts dictate varying strategies for different campaigns. For this reason, consultants generally view the ideal plan as one that provides money to the candidate, which can readily be converted into the precise resources he needs the most. Plans providing services (television time, mailing privileges, and so on) might offer benefits that candidates find less useful.

Despite this preference, consultants usually support plans advocating free or reduced-cost television time to candidates. Most consultants work in campaigns in which television time costs are a major expense. In these campaigns, free television services could be translated directly into cost relief. The consultant prefers that television time be given (free or at reduced cost) to the candidate without restrictions on his flexibility in using it. One veteran media consultant explained: "In other words, just *any* free time exposure is not what we're after. A panel show or an interview may be all right for some candidates. But others may show up better in some

29. See *Campaign Broadcast Reform Act of 1969*, Hearings before the Senate Committee on Commerce, 91 Cong. 1 sess. (1969), pp. 145–57.
30. See *New York Times*, Nov. 15, 1970.

other type of format. You have to use what your candidate does best at." Another commented: "A candidate and his manager like to show their strong suits. They like to avoid their weak ones." For these reasons, consultants rigorously examine broadcast time proposals for specifications pertaining to format, length of political appearances, and the use of advertising. The less a candidate's control over these three areas, the greater the prospect that he will appear less advantageously. Consultants vigorously guard against such circumscription.

BROADCASTERS

During the last half-century, broadcasting has grown from a few scattered radio stations into a large industry. Over 6,500 commercial radio stations and over 850 commercial television stations are now authorized to operate in the United States.[31] In 1968, television stations (and networks) produced revenue totaling more than $2.5 billion and a profit of nearly $500 million.[32] Commercial radio stations logged revenues of nearly $1 billion, which permitted profits in excess of $100 million.[33] Despite this generally profitable picture, there is considerable diversity within the industry. Stations range in size from the small, local radio station (frequently operating at low power during daylight hours) that produces little profit to the large, metropolitan area television station (frequently owned and operated by one of the three major networks) that produces large profits each year. And within the television industry over 100 stations earn more than $1 million in profit each year while others lose money (see Table 4).

Broadcasters have a particularly important stake in campaign finance reform proposals. Highly visible broadcasting costs are the major expense in national and most statewide campaigns. As the use of television increases, the pressure to initiate government

31. FCC, *35th Annual Report/Fiscal Year 1969*, p. 125. Many stations authorized to operate are not actually operating as yet.

32. *Ibid.*, p. 133.

33. *Ibid.*, p. 145. Revenue data for radio stations do not include FM stations operated independently from AM stations.

TABLE 4. Number of Television Stations Reporting Profit or Loss, by Amount, 1968[a]

Profit or loss, in dollars	Number of stations			Percent of all stations reporting
	VHF	*UHF*	*Total*	
Reported profits				
5 million and up	22	0	22	5.0
3 million–5 million	16	0	16	3.6
1.5 million–3 million	53	0	53	12.0
1 million–1.5 million	31	0	31	7.0
600,000–1 million	33	0	33	7.5
400,000–600,000	34	2	36	8.2
200,000–400,000	85	11	96	21.8
100,000–200,000	45	8	53	12.0
50,000–100,000	34	18	52	11.8
25,000–50,000	19	6	25	5.7
Less than 25,000	15	8	23	5.2
Total	387	53	440	
Reported losses				
Less than 10,000	7	3	10	7.7
10,000–25,000	4	2	6	4.6
25,000–50,000	9	6	15	11.5
50,000–100,000	12	11	23	17.7
100,000–200,000	16	14	30	23.1
200,000–400,000	10	12	22	16.9
400,000 and over	7	17	24	18.5
Total	65	65	130	

Source: Federal Communications Commission, *35th Annual Report/Fiscal Year 1969*, p. 136.

a. Some of the 680 operating stations did not report. In some instances figures for satellite stations were included in reports of the parent station.

action to require free or reduced-cost time intensifies. Broadcasters are especially vulnerable in such contests since the federal government grants franchises and regulates stations.

Most broadcasters have resisted any effort to impose federally directed requirements on electronic political advertising. They do so because they must compete with other media, notably newspapers and magazines, for the advertising dollar, and regulation of their rate structure could weaken their competitive position. They argue that if the government can set rates or specify rate reductions for one type of advertising in the public interest, reductions might extend to other types in the future as the concept of public interest expands. As one network executive explained, "If they could regulate this, there is no telling what might be next." If the public interest justifies cheaper advertising charges for political candidates, might it not justify the same for other good causes? Presumably it could, and a possibly lengthy list of such items haunts the broadcaster. His concern that government regulation could affect profit ledgers is not groundless. The federal government began prohibiting cigarette advertising on television in 1971. Broadcasters view this as lost revenue for them and probable profit for competing media. The industry is thus determined to protect its freedom to set political advertising time charges.

Broadcasters also usually oppose legislation that requires them to devote specified amounts of time to political advertising or political journalism, even if it requires no rate reduction. Unlike the printed media, the electronic media cannot add "space" at will. Their principal commodity—time—is fixed and limited. Once time has passed it is no longer usable. Industry codes and public pressures, moreover, reduce the amount available within any hour for commercial exploitation. Any government time requirement would likely displace commercial utilization of time, resulting in revenue loss for broadcasters. If electronic "space" could be added at will, such requirements would impose considerably less hardship on the station operator. But since this is not the case he fights to maintain his present control over his time. The more flexible this control, the more valuable the time to him.

Coupled with this, the candidate's demand for time is short term. It peaks in the fall of election years. At the same time the new program season and fall advertising campaigns combine to produce heavy private demand peaks. Candidates' advertising needs can produce headaches, as explained by a station manager: "Political advertising is really not needed by most television stations. We are glad to handle it—it improves our profit situation. But it's a short-term demand. They come in right at the time when demand for time is the highest. You sometimes have to preempt long-term advertisers. They complain about it, but have come to recognize the problem. You also have to be careful how much you sell one guy because you have to [sell] his opponent an equal amount of time if he wants it." Political advertising thus creates administrative difficulties for stations and frequently displaces regular advertisers. Some broadcasters contend that these supplanted advertisers may take their business elsewhere—notably to the printed media, which can create advertising space at will. Some of this business could remain lodged there, even when electronic space becomes available after the election. If the time once filled by political commercials is not replaced, broadcasters could suffer long-term revenue losses. Many broadcasters believe that plans that dictate reduced rates for political advertisers or prescribe time for political programs would further complicate their problems, increasing time demands on an already tight schedule. They would also reduce a station's flexibility to match the supply of time with demand, which could produce revenue losses.

Broadcasters frequently resist campaign finance plans that impose requirements on the industry because they do not believe that government regulation of the industry justifies interference in the private business of stations. A leading spokesman for broadcasters, summing up the views of many, declared: "The airwaves are not a public resource in the same way that some of the other natural resources are. [Reaches into air.] What's here? Nothing! With oil, you deplete it when you use it. Trees, land, all the rest. But we don't use airwaves up. . . . These companies developed the technological capacity to exploit it, government didn't. They buy the equipment to do this with, government doesn't. So I don't think there is much to this argument that the industry owes something in return, just because it is regulated and uses what some term a public resource." At least some broadcasters assign to government only the task of allocating broadcasting frequencies and protecting their integrity, without imposing additional encumbrances upon stations.

Even if government is justified in imposing requirements on the industry, broadcasters still resent reform plans that provide the services of one regulated industry (theirs) while neglecting those of others that candidates need during campaigns. A network executive contended: "The telephone company enjoys a monopoly at government direction. It also uses airwaves on its long-distance facilities. Airlines, newspapers, magazines—they all enjoy government benefits. So why shouldn't they also be asked to share this burden?"

For all these reasons, broadcasters generally resist any campaign finance proposals that affect political advertising.[34] The industry's main concern is to protect its present prerogatives while searching for solutions that will reduce mounting pressures to decrease the highly visible costs of television during campaigns.

The industry's interest in political broadcasting is bolstered by resources that give it great weight in the debate on campaign finance. Stations operate in every state and most congressional districts. Their managers and owners are respected in their local communities. They also dispense favors to elected officials. Many feature a senator or representative in a regular "Report from Washington." Officeholders, in addition, frequently feel, rightly or wrongly, that friendly relations with stations foster more favorable treatment on news shows and aid in buying more favorable time slots for spot advertising during campaigns. Broadcasters consequently have a friendly hearing in the halls of government.[35] The industry also supports a highly qualified staff at its National

34. See *Campaign Broadcast Reform Act of 1969*, Hearings, pp. 61–65, 103–36, 165–67, 183–92; *Projections—Predictions of Election Results and Political Broadcasting*, Hearings before the Senate Committee on Commerce, 90 Cong. 1 sess. (1967), pp. 135–72, 184–208, 228–307; and *Political Campaign Financing Proposals*, Hearings, pp. 481–85.

35. A congressional ethics study discounts the possibility that congressional ownership of broadcasting stations accounts for the industry's favorable treatment in Congress. It found that only a few members own interests in stations (although two of these sit on committees with jurisdiction over the Federal Communications Commission) and attributed favorable congressional reaction to broadcasters to members' dependence upon them for publicity and free time. See Report of the Association of the Bar of the City of New York Special Committee on Congressional Ethics, *Congress and the Public Trust* (Atheneum, 1970), pp. 54–55.

Association of Broadcasters headquarters in Washington, D.C. This organization keeps station members posted on government developments that affect them and can galvanize the membership for action when necessary.

THE FEDERAL COMMUNICATIONS COMMISSION

The Federal Communications Commission (FCC) is the major government agency that regulates the broadcasting industry. Assignment of signal frequency and strength is necessary because stations must use the scarce electromagnetic spectrum, which is in the public domain, to transmit their signals. Without regulation, signals might interfere with each other, making it impossible for stations to transmit programs that could be received clearly by home receivers. The seven-member commission in effect grants to individuals a three-year license to exploit the scarce airwaves for private benefit. In return, licensees must operate their stations in the "public interest, convenience, or necessity." This license and the obligations imposed by it are a principal justification for requiring broadcasters to provide free or reduced-cost time to candidates for public office.

The commission shares the characteristics of most regulatory agencies.[36] It has never been known for aggressive, innovative leadership. Its critics, led by Nicholas Johnson, one of the seven commissioners, claim that the industry it is supposed to regulate has captured it.[37] Broadcasters, however, frequently resent its interference in what they regard to be the personal business of private enterprise activities.

The FCC could lead in advocating changes in the industry that might reduce charges for political time. Federally directed change might also produce better news coverage of campaigns. The commission, however, hesitates to exert leadership in this area. One of its most influential members commented: "I don't see the FCC

36. See Marver Bernstein, *Regulating Business by Independent Commission* (Princeton University Press, 1955).

37. See Nicholas Johnson, *How to Talk Back to Your Television Set* (Little, Brown, 1970).

as playing a role in this. It is the prerogative of Congress." In the past the agency generally resisted proposals that went beyond voluntary station action.[38] Under its new chairman, Dean Burch, the commission may have reversed its long-standing hostility to federally imposed requirements related to time charges, however. In mid-1970 Burch indicated commission support for federal requirements that would reduce rates for political advertising, if the reductions applied to all candidates.[39]

The FCC prefers plans that permit easy administration, facilitating clear guidelines for license holders. Crucial to the guidelines are rules governing the eligibility of candidates for benefits, and the obligations of stations. Agency fear of administrative headaches has prompted past opposition, as indicated by the testimony of a former chairman, William E. Henry: "The volume and complexity of the complaints which can be anticipated if either S. 252 or S. 1696 [bills exempting several offices from the requirements of Section 315 of the Communications Act] is enacted raise a most important practical problem. It may be impossible for the Commission with its limited staff to settle many of them prior to the election."[40]

The FCC also has a penchant for voluntary station action and will undoubtedly be influenced by that in the future. Publicly, the commission favors modifying Section 315(a) of the Communications Act, the equal time rule, for presidential candidates. Some commissioners, in speeches to and conversations with broadcasters, also encourage stations to grant voluntary rate reductions to candidates, although to date they have neither specified nor suggested using the reduction as a criterion for determining license renewal.

38. See *Campaign Broadcast Reform Act of 1969*, Hearings, pp. 47–50, 67–82; *Equal Time*, Hearings before the Senate Committee on Commerce, 88 Cong. 1 sess. (1963), pp. 57–100; and *Projections—Predictions*, Hearings, pp. 84–114.

39. See *Political Broadcasting—1970*, Hearings before the House Committee on Interstate and Foreign Commerce, 91 Cong. 2 sess. (1970), pp. 7–31.

40. *Equal Time*, Hearings, p. 75; see also *Projections—Predictions*, Hearings, pp. 88–92.

REFORM GROUPS

Several groups have spearheaded the effort to change campaign finance. Most have no specific legislative interest but would fall into the general category of "good government" groups. The most visible of those presently active include the Committee for Economic Development, the Twentieth Century Fund, and the National Committee for an Effective Congress.[41] These groups share common concerns and objectives for campaign financing. They seek reform that would stimulate citizen participation in democratic processes, promote an informed citizenry, relieve financial pressure on candidates, and establish basic access to broadcast media.[42]

They enter the struggle burdened by several handicaps. Their opponents are geographically dispersed and possess grassroots strength; the reform groups draw their primary strength from the Eastern Seaboard. None organizes around a single economic activity that might activate its membership. None has a huge membership.[43] Only the National Committee for an Effective Congress (NCEC) has achieved notable legislative success; its proposal served as a basis for the 1970 campaign finance reform bill. Significantly, the NCEC contributes fairly sizable amounts to several congressional and senatorial candidates which facilitates its access to the legislative arena.

Reform group efforts, however, do not go wasted. These groups seek, among other things, to establish a climate favorable to campaign finance change. Legislators often borrow their ideas. And other groups, some with large, grassroots organizations, will likely join them in the future.

41. The proposals advanced by these groups and the arguments supporting them can be found in Twentieth Century Fund, *Voters' Time* and *Electing Congress;* CED, *Financing a Better Election System;* and *Campaign Broadcast Reform Act of 1969*, Hearings, pp. 1–3, 51–60, 82–90.

42. See Twentieth Century Fund, *Voters' Time*, p. 17; and CED, *Financing a Better Election System*, pp. 12–14.

43. The CED and Twentieth Century Fund have no membership per se, but are largely study organizations.

Conclusions

Interaction among participants in the campaign finance struggle resembles that in many areas where change is advocated. On the one hand several diffuse groups, with general, idealistic interests, demand reform (with proposals varying in emphasis and content). Discontinuity and disorganization plague their efforts. Arrayed against them are well-organized, established, specific-interest groups, backed by considerable resources. In the past, three such groups effectively blocked campaign finance reform.[44] Broadcasters wanted to avoid additional regulation; they opposed legislation that would require them to grant rate reductions or devote time to campaign coverage. Political parties, frequently torn by conflict, feared greater discord; some plans could enhance the power of one or another faction or organization. Elected officials felt that changes would diminish their advantages as incumbents.

Growing campaign costs, however, are eroding this coalition. Elected officials and party leaders (particularly Democratic leaders) are becoming increasingly willing to relinquish their fears in exchange for more adequate financing of campaigns. One campaign consultant explained the reaction of officials to increased costs: "They don't know how costly it has become. They're going to find when they go out [to campaign] again that they will have to look for money in some awfully strange places to get what's needed to wage a decent campaign today. I know. I've talked with them about what's needed. They're astounded!" The surest evidence that elected officials are reacting differently to finance reform is the passage by Congress of finance reform legislation in 1970 and 1971.

44. For a discussion of why organized groups frequently triumph over the diffuse groups, see Mancur Olson, Jr., *The Logic of Collective Action* (New York: Schocken Books, 1968), especially pp. 132–67.

Chapter Four

MAXIMIZING PARTICIPATION

THE DEMOCRAT cherishes and encourages widespread participation in the electoral process. A primary goal of campaign finance reform is to increase citizens' strength in that process and, through that, in public policy making. Reformers often assert that the fundamental changes they propose could expand participation by increasing access between candidates and voters, decreasing candidate dependence on rich contributors, and reducing barriers that discourage men without wealth from running for public office. It is difficult to quarrel with these goals, but it is easy to dispute whether the mechanisms advanced to accomplish them will work.

Competition for Office

Finance reform avowedly will make the quest for public office easier by reducing the financial barriers to campaigning for office. Private financing methods restrict entry to the contest and distort the odds even after a candidate gains entry. Reformers promote their plans as an answer to the democratic electoral imperative to present voters real alternatives at the polls. Finance change could strengthen political competition by encouraging more candidates to contest for office.

The goal of increasing access to the electoral arena is praiseworthy, but it could mean an uncontrolled proliferation of candidacies. There may be an ideal number of candidates contesting a given office beyond which voters become confused. The Twentieth Century Fund recognized the possibly adverse effects of proliferating candidacies in its broadcasting service plan: "But to provide Voters' Time to all legally qualified candidates might encourage the rise of irresponsible and disruptive candidates. It might fractionalize and factionalize the American political system. It would inevitably encourage the proliferation of splinter groups, provide publicity-seekers with an invaluable opportunity to attract nationwide attention on television and radio, and swamp the airwaves with a suffocating confusion of voices."[1]

The need for a balance between the benefits of stability and the opportunity to equalize contests for office was articulated by the Fund in its pursuit of finance reform: "What we do seek is the interplay of ideas—a healthy chance for the upward movement of new parties and candidates and the possible decline of the old, as well as the stability provided by a strong two-party system."[2] These twin objectives can be accomplished. The Fund's solution divides candidates into three categories, based on past electoral performance coupled with the opportunity for new parties to present petitions to qualify for some aid. It grants benefits to candidates somewhat in proportion to their demonstrated strength on the theory that under its formula an endless proliferation of candidacies is unlikely.

Incumbent officials, possessed of several strong advantages in the struggle for office, hesitate to equalize the contest or invigorate the opposition. Congressman Jim Wright of Texas, an advocate of campaign finance reform, typifies their reluctance: "Now, I should not want to encourage a thousand men in each district to come to the Treasury asking for money with which to run for office. I think it might have that effect if we expanded it into Senate and House races."[3] Most public officials seem more willing to provide

1. Twentieth Century Fund, *Voters' Time* (New York: Twentieth Century Fund, 1969), p. 20.
2. *Ibid.*, p. 21.
3. *Political Campaign Financing Proposals*, Hearings before the Senate Committee on Finance, 90 Cong. 1 sess. (1967), p. 269.

finance changes for other offices than for the one they hold. Opponents of reform sometimes play on incumbents' fears. Leonard Goldenson, president of the American Broadcasting Companies, for example, testified before a Senate subcommittee against a plan that would have provided television services to Senate and House candidates: "We should also recognize the possibility of additional candidates being encouraged to qualify for these contests just to be eligible for these spots and program time at such drastically reduced rates. I would guess that there would be a number of self-seekers who will take advantage of this opportunity—if available to them."[4]

Since reform proposals aim to invigorate the opposition and make it easier to contest for public office, there is no way to assuage the concern of incumbent officials. But increasing visibility of the difficulties of the present finance system may eventually force these officials to set aside their personal interest on campaign finance questions. Fund raising problems may also help to "convince" them to support reform. A veteran presidential campaign adviser explained: "Incumbents have an advantage and I know that congressmen in the past have been reluctant to vote advantages for themselves which their opponents can also take advantage of. But it is becoming so difficult even for incumbents to raise money that they are going to have to eventually come around."

Finance reform designed to maximize candidate participation might by offering candidates additional sources of funds (or services costing money) weaken already feeble political parties. It might also cause troubles between national party committees and other committees. Funds appropriated to national committees to distribute, for example, might offer them the opportunity to intervene in state and local contests almost with impunity. By using funds as rewards, national committees could alter basic competition patterns. Herbert Alexander, a campaign finance student, testified: "If the money is given to the national committee, this

4. *The Campaign Broadcast Reform Act of 1969*, Hearings before the Senate Committee on Commerce, 91 Cong. 1 sess. (1969), p. 124.

could significantly change power balances within the parties. I do not say it is necessarily wrong to give it to the national committee if you recognize that you are thereby strengthening the national committee vis-à-vis State and local committees or even vis-à-vis senatorial and congressional campaign committees."[5] Such a plan creates problems for those Democrats or Republicans who disagree with their national committees. Some types of plans present fewer problems than others. Appropriating public money directly to the party treasury, of course, raises the strongest possibility of strengthening national committees. Recent money and service plans, however, provide benefits directly to candidates.[6] Tax incentive plans also bypass the national party committee, leaving the basic allocation decision to the individual contributor.

These legitimate concerns about the impact of campaign finance change on competition for public office can be answered. Plans can be devised to provide candidates with enough money or services to wage at least a minimally effective campaign as well as to reduce the "entry fee" to the election arena.

Public Participation

INCREASING VOTERS' ACCESS TO CANDIDATES

If voters are to choose wisely, they need information about the choices confronting them. The democratic electoral process ideally informs voters about the issues at stake, spurs their interest in public affairs, and offers them a chance to express preferences among choices. But the present campaign financing method circumvents this process. Voters' ability to gather intelligence hinges more and more on candidates' ability to meet huge media expenses. Since individual resources vary, the system produces unequal and uneven information about office seekers. Only complete and some-

---

5. *Political Campaign Financing Proposals*, Hearings, p. 342.

6. Such plans could of course further decrease whatever little impact the parties presently have in the electoral process by making it possible for candidates to rely upon other sources for resources with which to wage their campaigns.

what equal information assures that the voter knows the choices
and that the preferences he expresses are based on adequate information. Worse yet, incomplete information may distort his
decision. Yet the present system provides no guarantee that voters
will receive even a basic minimum amount of campaign information.

Money consequently subverts the democratic electoral process.
Men of wealth determine which candidates voters will be able to
hear about. Campaign finance reform plans thus seek to facilitate
citizens' efforts to obtain information about office seekers. The
Twentieth Century Fund put the point succinctly: "It is our con-
viction that the strength of a democracy depends on a well-
informed electorate. . . . If the voter is to choose wisely, he needs
some guarantee of a basic access through the electronic media to all
significant candidates for our highest political offices." [7]

The Fund's Voters' Time plan went so far as to protect voter
access to candidates against the voter's own possible inclination to
the contrary. The plan would compel all broadcast facilities to
transmit proposed political programing simultaneously. During
these times, viewers' only alternative to the political programs
would be to turn off their sets. Although most plans seek to increase voters' access to the candidates, few go so far to "guarantee" access.

GUARANTEEING CANDIDATES' ACCESS TO VOTERS

The candidate's access to the voter is the other side of the coin.
Ideally, each candidate should have the opportunity to communicate his impressions about issues and his positions on them to the
voter. But again, the present financing method thwarts this process.
Candidates with solid financial backing can afford the media time
required to make their case; those without money can neither
make their case nor refute that of the opposition.

Promoters of change seek to assure candidates for public office
a minimum exposure to voters. As Senator Fred Harris, speaking

7. *Voters' Time*, p. 19.

as chairman of the Democratic National Committee, put it, "I do believe that the public would be much better served if every man started out saying, 'Whatever happens, I will at least have this minimum chance to get my message across.' "[8] Reformers also desire to free candidates from obligations—implicit or explicit— that hinder their discussion of all the issues and their taking the position they think best. Senator Russell Long, who drove the ill-fated 1966 Presidential Campaign Fund Act to passage, said that a candidate "should be permitted to make his campaign and have enough money to take his case to the people of this country and communicate his position to them without being beholden to anyone. . . . He ought to be in a position to take the stand he wants to take on matters vitally affecting all the people without regard to the financial consequences, and he ought to be able to communicate to the people what he believes and what he stands for without the pressure of these financial considerations bearing heavily upon him."[9]

As candidates and voters increasingly use the electronic media for communication, plans providing free or reduced-cost broadcast time can assure candidates the access they need.

INCREASING CITIZEN CONTROL OVER CANDIDATES

Shifting the campaign financing burden from individuals to other sources, as advocated in some reform proposals, is a matter of dispute. A shift could reduce the incentive of individuals to contribute (thus depriving them of a means to participate), diminish citizen control over candidates and officials, and decrease the incentive of political parties to pursue contributors.

Candidates and party activists believe that financial participation stimulates interest and enthusiasm among donors during campaigns. A U.S. senator explained: "Sometimes you try to raise money in small amounts. You do this not to meet expenses of your campaign so much as to expand the number who give to you. Once

8. *Campaign Broadcast Reform Act of 1969*, Hearings, p. 19.
9. *Political Campaign Financing Proposals*, Hearings, p. 170.

you have a guy who gives, you know he's going to vote for you and be interested in what you do. This is a very good way to build enthusiasm." When a person contributes to a candidate he does not remain a disinterested bystander. Shifting the finance burden could result in fewer people giving, either because they will feel less need to do so or because candidates and parties will not solicit their money as boldly as they do now.

Transferring campaign financing burdens from individuals could also remove from citizens' grasp one lever they can use to determine who runs for and holds office. Former Senator Joseph Tydings, supporting citizen control, once testified: "Parties should derive their financing because they have the support of the people, not because they have support of the government. In our free party system, political parties have grown and prospered according to the amount of public support they could command for their candidates and programs, not according to the amount they can cajole from the Congress."[10] Testifying on the same proposal, Senator Robert Kennedy commented: "To aid campaigns by direct subsidy from the Treasury would only further separate the individual citizen from the political process—insulating the party organization from any need to reach citizens, except through the one way communication of television and advertising. The political parties would talk to the citizen; but the individual could not talk back."[11] Both senators raised these possibilities while testifying against the Presidential Campaign Fund Act, which shifted the finance burden more drastically than did the 1970 reform bill passed by Congress (as well as most other broadcasting-centered proposals). But their argument is applicable to any plan that diminishes the place of

10. *Ibid.*, p. 413. Senator Tydings was later a leading promoter of a proposal that required stations to provide reduced-rate television time. This plan shifts the burden of financing, but not so drastically as that contemplated by the public subsidy bill he testified against.

11. *Ibid.*, pp. 247–48. The opposition of both Senators Kennedy and Tydings was prompted in part by their fear that the Democratic National Committee would use the funds accruing to it to finance President Johnson's reelection bid, thereby putting potential challengers at a disadvantage.

individual contributors in financing campaigns. This argument, of course, assumes that all citizens possess equal amounts of money with which to exercise control. Since this is not the case, only those who can afford to contribute benefit from this control.

Campaign finance reform could also decrease the possibility of widespread financial participation by reducing political parties' incentive to broaden the base of contributors. Parties may be lax in creating a broad base of givers under the present system; they would be even less likely to do so if they could turn to other sources for funds.

But none of the plans providing free or reduced-cost services give candidates all of the assistance they need. Since office seekers will need additional funds to pay for other necessary items, they will still have some incentive to solicit and encourage giving, and givers will have some incentive to give. Most plans providing money directly to candidates, moreover, provide for some form of public participation. The voucher plan permits the taxpayer to allocate public money to the candidate or party committee of his choice. Even the tax checkoff plans of 1966 and 1971 provide a form of participation (albeit a flimsy one) by giving taxpayers an opportunity to designate $1 of their taxes for national campaigns by checking an appropriate box on their tax return form. Tax credit and deduction plans specifically seek to promote wider participation through giving by establishing a monetary incentive to contribute.

It would not be disturbing if finance change should reduce the opportunity for citizen participation through giving. No more than 12 percent of the population contributes to candidates at all levels in most election years.[12] Since those who do give tend to be wealthier than those who do not, campaign financing provides the wealthy a route of access to office seekers and a means of extracting implicit commitments from them. The present finance system

12. See Alexander Heard, *The Costs of Democracy* (University of North Carolina Press, 1960), pp. 38–47; and Herbert E. Alexander, *Financing the 1964 Election* (Princeton, N.J.: Citizens' Research Foundation, 1966), p. 69.

provides the general electorate with little control over candidates and officeholders. It would be preferable to trade the present method and its participatory "benefits" for one that extends voter-candidate access, reduces financial barriers to office, and makes candidates less dependent upon the wealthy. It is measurably better, and a mark of wider participation, for officials to be chosen by votes, which are distributed relatively equally, than by money, which is not.

Free Time

Suspension of Section 315(a)—the equal time clause—of the Communications Act is not only the most frequently proposed means of providing services or money to candidates but also the only one that has been implemented recently. In 1960 Congress temporarily suspended this clause for presidential candidates during the general election period. It is possible therefore to judge its effectiveness in increasing candidates' access to voters and voters' access to candidates.

STATIONS' RESPONSE TO SUSPENDING SECTION 315(A)

Broadcasters who favor suspending Section 315(a) contend that they would provide more political programing, which would be educationally beneficial to voters, free of charge to major candidates if they were free of the obligation to provide comparable time to even the most minor candidates. Since 1959 the equal time requirement has not applied to newscasts, news interviews, or news documentaries. A candidate's appearance in exempt shows must, however, be "incidental to the presentation of the subject or subjects covered" by the program; otherwise the stations must grant equal opportunities to his opponents.

Suspension of Section 315(a) would give stations more freedom to augment campaign coverage; they could, for example, present documentaries focusing directly on candidates, initiate special coverage of the campaign outside of regular news programs, and provide time directly to candidates to make appearances as they choose.

The three major national television networks have been most explicit in their promise of time if the equal opportunities clause were suspended. They have pledged free time in prime evening hours to major presidential contestants in 1972, provided Congress suspends Section 315(a) for this office. NBC has offered four prime-time half-hours for appearances by the presidential and vice presidential candidates of the major parties.[13] The other networks are vague about the time they would grant, but past practices would presumably guide them in 1972. In 1964, CBS offered time weekly during the eight weeks prior to the election. Assuming one thirty-minute program per candidate, this offer would have totaled at least eight hours. The 1960 debates, moreover, totaled approximately four hours. Suspending Section 315(a) could thus be expected to produce between four and eight hours of prime time on each network, free of charge to major presidential candidates.

The networks claim that presidential candidates can make the principal decisions about how to use free time. Chairman John Pastore of the Senate communications subcommittee, while defending the suspension of Section 315(a) for presidential candidates contained in the 1970 reform bill, stated, "My understanding is that [the networks] have pledged that they will give 30-minute segments—several of them—over to the candidate, and that the format will be at the choosing of the candidate."[14] Indeed, NBC's offer for 1972 specifically states that the time is "for use as [the candidates] see fit."[15] One network executive contended that "the networks have always been willing to negotiate format." Another stated, "I don't think that we can ever get into a position of telling

13. *Projections—Predictions of Election Results and Political Broadcasting*, Hearings before the Senate Committee on Commerce, 90 Cong. 1 sess. (1967), p. 154; and *Political Broadcasting—1970*, Hearings before the House Committee on Interstate and Foreign Commerce, 91 Cong. 2 sess. (1970), p. 88.

14. *Congressional Record* (daily ed.), April 14, 1970, p. S5717.

15. *Projections—Predictions*, Hearings, p. 154; and *Political Broadcasting—1970*, Hearings, p. 88.

an incumbent president, or even candidates for that matter, how they're going to use their time." The president of CBS testified, "There are a variety of formats we can provide for candidates if given the freedom, if we have the choice to take only the principal [candidates]."[16]

Despite this generosity, broadcasters strongly prefer a "debate" format that highlights confrontation between the contenders. They believe that face-to-face encounters attract large audiences, and they cite the 1960 experience to prove their point. One network executive after stating a willingness to negotiate format explained: "But we believe that debates like we presented in 1960 would be the best way. We want to get away from these deathly thirty minute candidate talk shows. They lose audiences. And then you don't have anyone watching the regular commercial shows which must pay the bill." Another commented: "Now we would like to see interesting programs with some educational value to the public. The 1960 format proved to be interesting. It drew huge audiences." And another agreed: "No one is absolutely wedded to the debate format. But most people think there would be some excitement in this confrontation. Putting a guy on with a mike is about the most deadly thing you can do."

Broadcasters argue that debate generates high-quality information that voters find useful. As one put it: "But we do basically prefer debates. They draw out the candidates. They show issue positions. They highlight their personalities. All of this is important." Another commented: "We have pushed for debates because we believe they are in the public interest. What better way for the voter to compare candidates than when they are side by side?" And a third executive exulted that the 1960 debates "for the first time let a candidate's partisans receive some exposure to the opposing candidates." Debates, furthermore, spark voters' interest in elections, stirring their efforts to learn about candidates and broadening participation in the electoral process. CBS President Frank Stanton approvingly quoted public opinion polls to support his efforts to have the 1960 suspension of Section 315(a) repeated:

16. *Projections—Predictions*, Hearings, p. 297.

"Public-opinion polls revealed that those 'very much interested' in the campaign rose from 45 per cent before the debates to 57 per cent after them, compared with a rise, during a like period in 1956, from 46 per cent to only 47 per cent. And on Election Day, 1960, 64.5 per cent of eligible voters went to the polls as compared with 60.4 per cent four years earlier."[17]

If candidates accept a debate format similar to the one used in 1960, the networks would again permit them great freedom to outline the details. One who negotiated the 1960 network arrangements for candidate Richard Nixon commented, "I felt under absolutely no pressure from the networks and didn't feel at any time that I had to accept something I didn't want." A network executive lamented: "A good many politicians feel that we have forced debates on the candidates. This has not been the case at all. We wanted real debates in 1960, but the representatives of the candidates ended up getting most of the control over those programs."

If candidates should not accept a debate format for 1972, the networks would probably agree, with some reluctance, to other types of presentations.

THE RESTRAINTS OF SECTION 315

If Section 315(a) induces broadcasters to limit the free time they provide candidates, then stations should be more generous when freed from its constraints. When the equal time rule was suspended for presidential candidates in 1960, radio and television network free-time offerings to the candidates and their supporters increased by more than 20 percent over 1956, as indicated by Figure 6. Since 1960, free time has declined sharply, particularly on television networks. Most of the free time provided by networks presumably goes to presidential candidates, so that equal time restrictions could sharply curtail the amount of time they receive.

The amount of free time that presidential candidates themselves have received on the networks is shown in Figure 7. Time pro-

17. Frank Stanton, "The Case for Political Debates on TV," *New York Times Magazine*, Jan. 19, 1964, p. 16.

FIGURE 6. Free Time Provided Candidates and Their
Supporters by Television and Radio Networks, General
Elections, 1956–68[a]

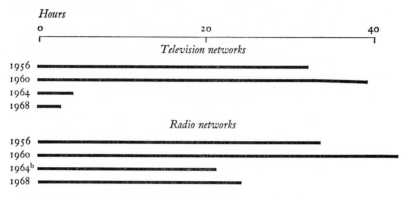

Sources: Federal Communications Commission (FCC), *Survey of Political Broadcasting,
1960*, Table 10; *1964*, Table 4; *1968*, Table 4. *1956 General Election Campaigns*, Report of
the Subcommittee on Privileges and Elections to the Senate Committee on Rules and Administration, 85 Cong. 1 sess. (1957), Exhibit 24, p. 5 (cited hereafter as Gore Committee
Report).

a. Figures for 1956 and 1960 cover the period from Sept. 1 to general election date and
could include some primary campaigns.

b. Does not include FM stations programed separately from AM stations.

vided to presidential candidates (but not counting time given to
persons appearing on their behalf) actually declined from 1956 to
1960, despite removal of equal time requirements in the presidential contest in 1960. The decrease is due to the much smaller
amount of time granted minor party aspirants; major party candidates' time remained fairly stable, as the following list of time
provided (in hours and minutes) indicates:[18]

	Television		Radio	
	1956	*1960*	*1956*	*1960*
Democratic party	8:25	8:06	9:03	10:48
Republican party	10:43	8:06	11:11	10:18
Other parties	10:30	1:20	11:45	0:51

18. *1956 General Election Campaigns*, Report of the Subcommittee on Privileges
and Elections to the Senate Committee on Rules and Administration, 85 Cong. 1 sess.
(1957), Exhibit 24, p. 5; Federal Communications Commission (FCC), *Survey of
Political Broadcasting, 1960*, Table 14.

FIGURE 7. Network and Commercially Sponsored Time
Provided Free on Television and Radio Networks to Presidential
Candidates, General Elections, 1956–68[a]

Dark areas represent commercially sponsored time where reported separately

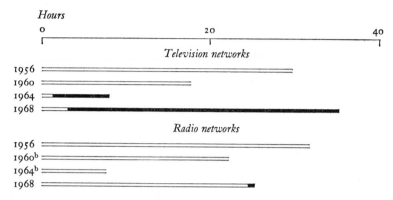

Sources: FCC, *Survey of Political Broadcasting, 1960,* Table 14; *1964,* Table 5; *1968,*
Table 5. Gore Committee Report, Exhibit 24, p. 5.

a. Figures for 1956 and 1960 cover the period from Sept. 1 to general election date and
could include some primary campaigns. Figures for 1968 include time for supporters.

b. Does not include FM stations programed separately from AM stations.

The dramatic debates of 1960 sharply focused attention on the free
time that networks provided presidential candidates that year, thus
obscuring the decline in total free time. Neither before nor since
have free time programs approached the same level of visibility.

Free time declined even more sharply between 1960 and 1964
(when equal time requirements once again applied) than in the
previous four years. Free time totals once again surged upward
between 1964 and 1968, largely as the result of vastly increased
amounts of commercially sponsored free time on television network programs. By 1968 the amount of free time provided candidates once again approached the 1956 level.

Broadcasters' past performance suggests that if stations had been
freed from all equal time restraints the free time presented to presidential candidates would have increased even more than it has. The
strong upsurge in 1968 is almost entirely due to programing
already exempt from equal time restrictions—regularly scheduled

news programs and interview shows. Section 315(a) does pose formidable barriers to networks and stations by compelling them to offer the same amount of time to minor contenders that they grant to major ones. In recent elections the number of individuals contesting the presidency has been large (as shown in Table 5), rarely dropping below one dozen. If equal time requirements were suspended completely, stations could offer candidates free time on a more flexible basis than is now possible. This could increase the amount of free time they grant presidential candidates, thus increasing candidates' access to voters.

Suspending Section 315 would probably produce less free time for candidates of minor parties unless they were likely to receive a substantial vote. Minor parties, for example, received much less time in 1960 than in 1956, but there were no candidates then likely to receive a large vote. In 1968, however, when the American Independent party candidate George Wallace ran for the presidency, minor party candidates did receive as much time, in programing exempt from Section 315(a) requirements, as did the candidates of the major parties.

Suspending Section 315(a) does not guarantee a larger absolute amount of free time for presidential candidates. When it was suspended in 1960, the amount of time received by presidential candidates dropped from the 1956 level.

Competition patterns for other offices differ drastically from that for the presidency. Broadcasters contend that they are willing to provide time to two candidates but are unwilling to provide it for more than two. Most House and Senate contests attract only two candidates in the general elections, as shown by Table 6 (although 1968 produced a flurry of contests with more than two aspirants). Section 315(a) should therefore impose no barriers to stations providing time to these candidates.[19] Broadcasters' reports to the Federal Communications Commission, however, show that

19. Stations might assert that Section 315(a) restrains them from offering free time since it could encourage additional candidates in a future election. They would still be free in that future election, however, to refuse to offer free time.

TABLE 5. Candidates and Parties on Presidential Ballots, 1952–68[a]

Election year	Candidates	Parties
1952	Dwight D. Eisenhower	Republican
	Adlai E. Stevenson	Democratic
	Vincent Hallinan	Progressive American Labor
	Stuart Hamblen	Prohibition
	Eric Hass	Socialist Labor
	Darlington Hoopes	Socialist
	Farrell Dobbs	Socialist Workers
	Douglas MacArthur	American First Constitution
	Daniel J. Murphy	American Vegetarian
	Homer A. Tomlinson	Church of God
	Frederick P. Proehl	Greenback
	Henry B. Krajewski	Poor Man's
1956	Dwight D. Eisenhower	Republican
	Adlai E. Stevenson	Democratic Liberal
	T. Coleman Andrews	States Rights Constitution Independent
	Enock A. Holtwick III	Prohibition
	Eric Hass	Socialist Labor Industrial Government Independent
	Darlington Hoopes	Independent Socialist Virginia Socialist Democratic
	Harry Flood Byrd	Independent States Rights States Rights Party of Kentucky South Carolinians for Independent Electors
	Farrell Dobbs	Socialist Workers Militant Workers Independent
	William E. Jenner	Texas Constitution
	Henry Krajewski	American Third
	William Langer	Pioneer
	Herbert M. Shelton	American Vegetarian

TABLE 5. *Continued*

Election year	Candidates	Parties
1956	Frederick C. Proehl	Greenback
	Gerald L. K. Smith	Christian Nationalist
1960	John F. Kennedy	Democratic
	Richard M. Nixon	Republican
	C. Benton Coiner	Conservative Party of Virginia
	Merritt Curtis	Constitution
	Lar Daly	Tax Cut
	R. L. Decker	Prohibition
	Farrell Dobbs	Socialist Workers
		Farmer Labor Party of Iowa
		Socialist Workers and Farmers
	Orval E. Faubus	National States Rights
	Symon Gould	American Vegetarian
	Eric Hass	Socialist Labor
		Industrial Government
	Clennon King	Afro-American Unity
	Henry Krajewski	American Third
	J. Bracken Lee	Conservative Party of New Jersey
	Whitney Harp Slocomb	Greenback
	William Lloyd Smith	American Beat Consensus
	Charles Sullivan	Constitution Party of Texas
	[No designated candidate]	Independent American
1964	Barry M. Goldwater	Republican
	Lyndon B. Johnson	Democratic
	Eric Hass	Socialist Labor
	Clifton DeBerry	Socialist Workers
	E. Harold Munn	Prohibition
	Kirby J. Hensley	Universal
	John Kasper	National States Rights
	Joseph B. Lightburn	Constitution
	[No designated candidate]	Conservative
1968	Richard M. Nixon	Republican
	Hubert H. Humphrey	Democratic
	George C. Wallace	American Independent
		Independent
		Courage
		American
		George Wallace's
	E. Harold Munn	Prohibition

Election year	*Candidates*	*Parties*
1968	Eugene McCarthy	New Party (and write-ins)
	Eldridge Cleaver	Peace and Freedom New Politics
	Fred Halstead	Socialist Workers
	Henning A. Blomen	Socialist Labor
	Dick Gregory	New Party (Peace and Freedom)
	Charlene Mitchell	Communist
	Kent M. Soeters	Berkeley Defense Group
	Kirby J. Hensley	Universal
	Ventura Chavez	Peoples Constitutional
	Richard K. Troxell	Constitution
	[No designated candidate]	Peace and Freedom Electors
	[No designated candidate]	New Reform Electors
	[No designated candidate]	New Party Electors

Sources: Congressional Quarterly Service, *Historical Review of Presidential Candidates from 1788 to 1968* (Washington: Congressional Quarterly Service, 1969), pp. 20–21; Richard M. Scammon (ed.), *America at the Polls* (University of Pittsburgh Press, 1965), pp. 18–20; *Report (To Accompany S. 3637)*, Senate Committee on Commerce, 91 Cong. 2 sess. (1970), p. 3; *Congressional Quarterly Weekly Report*, Special Supplement, Vol. 27 (June 6, 1969).

a. Each candidate or party was the choice of a slate of electors in at least one state. State laws do not uniformly require that presidential candidates to whom electors' votes are pledged be identified nor do most states bind electors' pledges.

stations are no more likely to provide time to candidates for U.S. senator and state governor in two-way races than to those in three-way (or more) races, as shown in Figure 8. In 1968, stations were actually more likely to provide time to candidates in the larger races.[20] FCC data do not provide records for other offices below the presidency.

Individual stations have been granting all candidates increasing amounts of free time since 1956, with the most dramatic surge occurring between 1956 and 1960, as shown by Figure 9. That increase was probably due not to the equal time suspension of that year but exemption of certain programing from equal time rules in the previous year. In fact, most of the long-term growth in free time is the result of increases in the amount of time that stations

20. FCC data show only the number of stations offering free time rather than the amount of time each station offered.

TABLE 6. Number of Contestants for Seats in U.S. Senate and House Elections, 1958–68

Election year	Senate contests with						House contests with					
	1 candidate		2 candidates		3 or more candidates		1 candidate		2 candidates		3 or more candidates	
	Number	Percent of total	Number	Percent of total	Number	Percent of total	Number	Percent of total	Number	Percent of total	Number	Percent of total
1958	0	0.0	33	97.1	1	2.9	90	20.7	331	76.1	14	3.2
1960	0	0.0	30	88.2	4	11.8	79	18.1	345	78.9	13	3.0
1962	1	2.6	38	97.4	0	0.0	57	13.1	378	86.9	0	0.0
1964	1	2.9	34	97.1	0	0.0	39	9.0	396	91.0	0	0.0
1966	3	8.6	29	82.9	3	8.6	53	12.2	360	82.8	22	5.1
1968	2	5.9	25	73.5	7	20.6	44	10.1	281	64.6	110	25.3

Sources: *Congressional Quarterly Weekly Report*, Vol. 16, No. 46 (Nov. 14, 1958), pp. 1450–56, 1460; Vol. 18, No. 47 (Nov. 18, 1960), pp. 1887–93, 1899; Vol. 20, No. 44 (Nov. 2, 1962), pp. 2092–95; Vol. 22, No. 43 (Oct. 23, 1964), pp. 2520–24; Vol. 24, No. 45, Pt. I (Nov. 11, 1966), pp. 2786, 2792–2802; Vol. 26, No. 45 (Nov. 8, 1968), p. 3084; Vol. 26, No. 46 (Nov. 15, 1968), pp. 3162–67.

FIGURE 8. Television Stations Providing Free Time in General Election Contests for Senator and Governor, by Number of Contestants, 1960–68

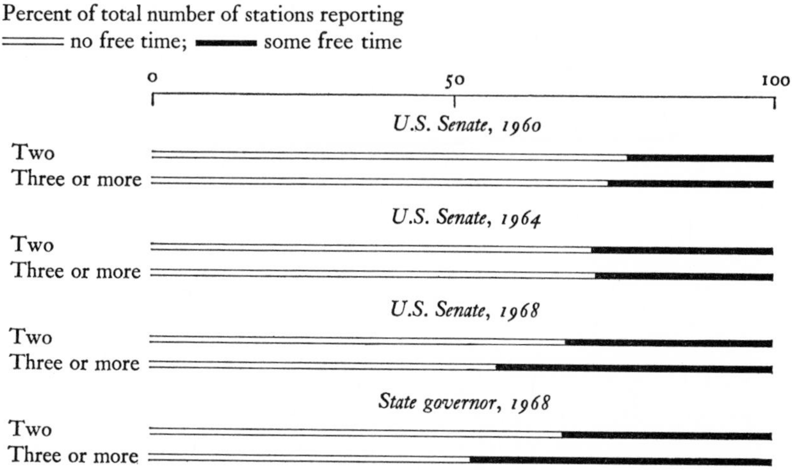

Percent of total number of stations reporting
===== no free time; ▬▬▬ some free time

Sources: FCC, *Survey of Political Broadcasting, 1960; 1964*, p. vii; *1968*, Table 16.

provide candidates on commercially sponsored programs, which are often local news programs that do not fall under the restraints of Section 315(a). Although the total hours appear to be very high, particularly in 1968, they represent the efforts of over 600 commercial television stations and over 2,500 commercial radio stations. The average station still provides very little free time, exclusive of network programing, to candidates.

Equal time requirements obviously do not offer substantial restraints to stations' coverage of election contests below the presidency. If Section 315 imposed the barriers that broadcasters claim it does, stations would be more likely to provide time to candidates in two-way races than to those in contests with more than two candidates. But they do not. Most stations do not provide time to candidates below the presidency for reasons other than equal time requirements.

Suspending Section 315(a) is therefore likely to offer more relief to presidential candidates than to any others. Numbers do restrain

FIGURE 9. Station and Commercially Sponsored Time
(Exclusive of Network Programing) Provided Free to All
Candidates on Television and Radio Stations, General
Elections, 1956–68[a]

Dark areas represent commercially sponsored time

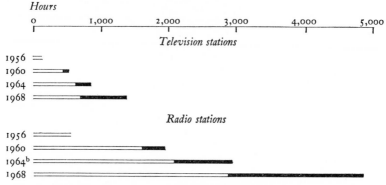

Sources: FCC, *Survey of Political Broadcasting, 1960*, Tables 26, 27a, 27b; *1964*, Tables 17, 30; *1968*, Tables 14, 25. Gore Committee Report, Exhibit 24, pp. 1, 15, 17.

a. Figures for 1956 and 1960 cover the period from Sept. 1 to general election date and could include some primary campaigns.

b. Does not include FM stations programed separately from AM stations.

stations from offering time to presidential candidates; they make little difference in whether stations provide time to candidates for lesser offices. As a station manager put it, "If Section 315 were changed, it would primarily have an impact on us at the national level. As it is now the networks are strapped because they cannot give time to the two major [presidential] candidates, because there are so many candidates from the Vegetarian and this and that party."

Some broadcasters would dispute this conclusion. For example, of 85 television station managers responding to a questionnaire, 45 (52.9 percent) indicated that if the Section 315 requirement to provide time to minor contenders were lifted, they would provide more time to local contests with wide interest, 38 (44.7 percent) would give more time to candidates for statewide and federal office, and 30 (35.3 percent) more time to presidential candidates; only 20 (23.5 percent) indicated they would not likely give more time to any candidate.[21] Other broadcasters, in personal interviews, contended that if public policy trusted them to grant more time to candidates for lesser offices, they would do so. But stations' past performance at levels below the presidency casts doubt upon these claims.

THE EDUCATIONAL VALUE OF DEBATES

In addition to increasing candidate access to voters, free time could increase voters' access to candidates by offering programing that instructs the voting public. Those who advocate suspending Section 315(a) often contend that the 1960 debates helped educate the voter. Extolling the benefits of debates, Robert W. Sarnoff, former board chairman of NBC, testified, "Relieved temporarily from the equal-time restriction of the Communications Act, the television and radio networks were able to present the two major candidates in a series of face-to-face encounters that permitted the American public to take unprecedented measure of their potential national leaders."[22] Do debates provide the high quality instruction that broadcasters claim for them?

Debates undoubtedly attract large audiences. National surveys show that about 65 percent of American adults viewed the first debate in 1960. At least two national surveys (Nielsen and Sindlinger) indicate that the audience drop-off for successive debates was small—about 5 percent—which suggests that debates continue to attract large audiences even after they are no longer a novelty.[23] Their broad appeal is one of the reasons why broadcasters prefer

21. Responses to question 7 of the Brookings broadcast questionnaire (see Appendix): "If Section 315 were changed in order that stations would not have to give time to fringe candidates, what would be the likely reaction of your station? (Check as many as applicable)" One respondent indicated the reaction would vary according to conditions and three indicated no opinion.

22. *Equal Time*, Hearings before the Senate Committee on Commerce, 88 Cong. 1 sess. (1963), p. 100.

23. For a summary of debate audience surveys, see Sidney Kraus (ed.), *The Great Debates* (Indiana University Press, 1962), pp. 188–89.

debates. Large audiences may also provide advantages to candidates, as one writer notes: "From the candidates' point of view there is an enormous gain too—in the ratio of $3\frac{1}{2}$ to 1—in sheer quantitative values favoring debates over the conventional political set speeches. Or putting it another way, the average paid political broadcast of the half-hour, night-time network variety attracted approximately 30 percent of the audience of the average debate. The debate audiences, despite their vast size, were unusual also in the extent to which they stayed with the hour-long debates."[24] Since attracting audiences is the first requisite of transmitting information, this capability supplies debates a notable asset.

Debates provide the opportunity for partisans to see and hear the message of the opposition. Side-by-side comparisons of candidates by an audience are impossible in the usual format. Voters usually pay little attention to the messages of candidates they oppose, hearing only the message of candidates they tend to support in the first place. Voter exposure to the "other side," no matter how minimal, would inform the voting decision.

Broadcasters contend that debate formats stimulate voters' interest in the campaign. They cite polling data that show more people were interested in the 1960 campaign than either the 1952 or 1956 campaign.[25] Survey Research Center data validate this claim; they also show that interest in the campaigns (measured by responses to a recurring question)[26] continued to increase throughout the sixties:

24. Frank Stanton, "A CBS View," in *ibid.*, p. 68.

25. For other supporting evidence, see Elihu Katz and Jacob J. Feldman, "The Debates in the Light of Research: A Survey of Surveys," in *ibid.*, p. 193.

26. In response to the question "Would you say that you have been very much interested, somewhat interested, or not much interested in following the political campaigns so far this year?" Survey Research Center, *The 1952 Election Study*, rev. ed. (Inter-University Consortium for Political Research [ICPR], University of Michigan, 1952), pp. 29–30; SRC, *The 1956 Election Study*, rev. ed. (ICPR, 1968), p. 53; SRC, *The 1960 Election Study*, rev. ed. (ICPR, 1970); SRC, *The 1964 Election Study*, rev. ed. (1971), p. 84; and *Intermediate Codebook 1968 Election Study* (1969), p. 60. Based on 1,899 responses in 1952, 1,762 responses in 1956, 1,954 in 1960, 1,571 in 1964, and 1,673 in 1968. Figures rounded to nearest tenth. Percentages do not total 100 because some responses are listed as "no answer" or "don't know."

	Percent of total				
Response	*1952*	*1956*	*1960*	*1964*	*1968*
Very much interested	34.5	29.5	36.9	38.1	38.4
Somewhat interested	31.9	39.4	36.6	36.5	40.1
Not much interested	26.9	30.6	24.7	25.0	20.7

This may indicate that increasing the possibility of exposure to the campaign through television (as measured by the increased number of homes with television sets and the increased use of television by candidates) can raise interest in the campaign, regardless of the program format. The higher levels of interest in the contests in the 1960s are not reflected in an increasing voter turnout, as the following percentages of the civilian voting age population that cast ballots in presidential elections between 1940 and 1968 show:[27]

Year	*Percentage turnout*	*Year*	*Percentage turnout*
1940	59.2	1956	60.1
1944	52.9	1960	64.0
1948	51.3	1964	62.9
1952	62.6	1968	61.8

The 1960 debates did increase interest in the campaign, but other kinds of television exposure apparently would have done the same. And though the increased interest has not increased voting turnout, it has probably encouraged voters to gather information more persistently. Thus the 1960 electorate was probably better informed than it would have been without the debates.

Twenty-seven percent of the respondents in one study reported that the 1960 encounters helped them learn something about the issues and 35 percent said they learned something about the candidates.[28] A number of studies of the 1960 debates also found that the audience watching or hearing them could recall candidates' positions on various issues with some facility.[29] But the most pervasive information transmitted through the debates was the

---

27. U.S. Bureau of the Census, *Statistical Abstract of the United States, 1969*, p. 368.
28. Katz and Feldman, in *ibid.*, p. 202.
29. *Ibid.*, pp. 200–05.

candidates' performance. Elihu Katz and Jacob I. Feldman, after analyzing the Roper polling data concerning the 1960 debates, concluded that a "candidate's general informedness and his style of presentation of facts and arguments were more important criteria for judgment than either what he said or his personality as a whole. . . . The Roper data seem to argue that style of presentation was more important than either the content of the presentation (issues) or the personality of the debater (image)."[30]

Katz and Feldman also report on a Canadian Broadcasting Corporation study that posed questions in such a fashion that the respondent could choose to talk about what the candidates said, about the men themselves, or about how they performed. The respondents emphasized candidates and their performances to the exclusion of the subject matter of the debates. The study concluded that a "television debate of this kind, which focuses attention so sharply on the contestants themselves, leaves a mass audience with . . . some very distinct impressions of the capabilities of the two men as debaters and as persons, but . . . with very little idea of what the debate was all about."[31] The debate format puts a premium on a candidate's appearing decisive by responding quickly and convincingly. He must above all appear to have the correct response in all matters. Debates thus do not guarantee thoughtful responses that communicate substantive knowledge.

Some critics argue that direct debates would provide more satisfactory educational experiences than did the modified debates of 1960. They feel that because the candidates were questioned by a panel of journalists, an element of artificiality hampered communication between Nixon and Kennedy. More traditional debates might transmit more information to voters. But the characteristics of the television medium itself—its notable success in transmitting impressions and style—intervene. Even with a traditional debate format, voters would probably learn more about a candidate's performance than about substantive issues.

30. *Ibid.*, p. 200.
31. Quoted from *ibid.*, p. 200.

A decided disadvantage of debates is candidates' unwillingness to appear in them. Congress did not renew the suspension of Section 315 for presidential candidates in either 1964 or 1968 because Candidate Lyndon Johnson did not want debates in 1964 and Candidate Richard Nixon did not want them in 1968. Even if the equal time requirement were again suspended for 1972, nothing guarantees that presidential aspirants will agree to appear.

Better known candidates or those faring better in a campaign avoid debates because they fear such confrontations will attract audiences for the benefit of their opponents. Senator John Pastore commented, "Mr. Eisenhower, at the time of the campaign against Adlai Stevenson, when he was invited to debate, said, 'Why should I give exposure to a man who is not as well known as I am?' "[32] When the front runner is also better financed than his opponent, he has double reason to deny exposure to his adversary. He does not want to furnish him time that he might not otherwise be able to afford. And when a major third party appears on the presidential scene, the front runner's calculations about the desirability of debates become more complicated. If debates had transpired in 1968, American Independent party candidate George Wallace would probably have participated in some of them. Nixon's agreement to debate would have generated free time and exposure for the third party candidate. An adviser to the 1968 Nixon campaign feared other consequences as well: "Firstly, the two major parties would have given the American party an element of respectability by bringing them under our umbrella. Second, [Wallace] could have been irresponsible. When you have two men, either of whom might be president, you can cut each other up. But knowing that you may have to govern the country within a very short time constrains you from saying things that would make that job impossible. Wallace would have tried to fan the flames to get another few points—even tenths of points—for his total. This would not have been a desirable consequence."

Candidates also detest debates because the format is out of their

32. *Equal Time*, Hearings, p. 49.

control. A veteran adviser to presidential candidates pointed to the risks: "You can make one mistake—have just one bad night—and it will cost you the election. Nixon showed this to be the case in 1960." Another old hand in presidential politics stated: "It's rarely mentioned, but an opponent may not want to debate either. He debates an incumbent president on foreign policy only at his peril, because an incumbent can always go back to secret information, tell about secret negotiations, or hint that there is a secret answer and if the challenger only had the information he wouldn't have been so stupid as to raise the question. Or he can simply say that we've tried that and it won't work." Because of the risks imposed by debates, as Herbert Alexander once explained, "many candidates are simply not willing to confront either an opponent or an issue, even to get free time."[33]

Suspending Section 315(a) thus provides no guarantee that voters' access to candidates will increase. Candidates may refuse to accept free time, particularly if networks advance their offers on a take-it-or-leave-it basis, specifying a debate format.

Debates as an educational tool should not be lightly discarded. They do offer higher quality information than any presently used alternative formats. One scholar after appraising the 1960 debates concluded that they have "some tendency to overcome the inclination—often remarked—of campaigners to say little about method and much about goals."[34] Suspending Section 315(a) could consequently guarantee voters more access to high-quality information about candidates. A suspension could also help assure that each major candidate would have some chance of getting his message to the voter. Thus some of the difficulties of the present finance system, particularly for presidential candidates, could be overcome.

OPPOSITION TO SUSPENDING SECTION 315(A)

Not all the effects of suspending the equal time clause would be beneficial. Although suspension promises to expose voters to more

33. *Political Broadcasting—1970*, Hearings, p. 94.
34. Stanley Kelley, Jr., "Campaign Debates: Some Facts and Issues," *Public Opinion Quarterly*, Vol. 26 (Fall 1962), p. 361. Kelley's appraisal (pp. 351–66) is generally very favorable toward debates.

information about major candidates, it could reduce their exposure to a variety of candidates. Section 315 was designed to guarantee equal access to the public airwaves; reformers advocate its repeal so that broadcasters may grant free time to major party candidates without obligation to minor parties. The Socialist Labor party, which regularly fields presidential candidates in several states, consistently opposes suspending the equal time rule. Their testimony before a U.S. Senate committee illustrates this difficulty:

> For this reason, it is of the utmost importance that these modern media of mass communication be kept open for the widest possible discussion of problems facing us and their possible solutions, particularly during campaigns for public office when the public mind is most alert to a consideration of these vital subjects. Where these media are restricted, or operated in such manner as to deny the people the full opportunity to hear and consider all serious views on the unprecedented questions of paramount importance to all of us, then democracy itself has been debauched, and an act of usurpation, intended or not, has been committed. . . .
>
> . . . The amendment, repeal or suspension of section 315(a) would not only hinder the growth and effectiveness of those minority parties already in existence, it would also inhibit the emergence of new political parties claiming to represent ideas and plans for improved or superior forms of government . . . which [the Declaration of Independence] declared to be the right and duty of citizens to present for adoption by the people. . . .
>
> . . . The Socialist Labor Party of America declares that the real question comes down to this: Do the American people have the right to hear all sides of the throbbing social, political, and economic issues of the day? We hold that they do, and that, indeed, they must hear all sides if they are to vote and act intelligently. The opponents of section 315(a) [who support suspending or modifying it] say, in effect, that they do not have this right. Their contentions amount to saying that the American people have the right, or the need, to hear only the candidates of the major parties; candidates, that is to say, who hold substantially identical views on all the vital social, political, and economic questions of our age.[35]

35. *Equal Time*, Hearings, pp. 146–48. For a black leader's view of the protection that Section 315(a) affords minority groups, see *Campaign Broadcast Reform Act of 1969*, Hearings, p. 183.

Broadcasters who advocate suspension challenge the claim that minor parties would not be treated fairly if Section 315 were lifted. They argue that equal time requirements restrain them from offering free time to any presidential candidates, including those of minor parties. They contend that without the equal time rule they would provide time to minor party candidates, although they grant that major party candidates would receive substantially more time than they presently receive. The leader of at least one minor party, the Conservative Party of New York State, agrees with broadcasters: "We discovered, moreover, that the existence of the equal opportunity requirement actually disadvantaged the minority parties through the production of a naturally overcautious attitude on the part of the broadcasters. Instead of giving full publicity to the minor parties, and to the interest they inspired, the broadcasters in fact extended the bare minimum time required, and nothing more, in order to avoid legal complications."[36]

The records of the free time that national radio and television networks granted to minor party presidential candidates during the last four general elections partially substantiate the fear that suspending Section 315 would reduce the amount of time received by those candidates. Between 1956 and 1960 the amount of time granted minor party candidates fell dramatically (see Figure 10). Of course, these office seekers fared no better in 1964, when Section 315 was operative, than they did in 1960, when it was not. But they did receive more time in both 1956 and 1968, when the equal time rule prevailed, than they did in 1960. There is thus a high probability that broadcasters would provide less time to presidential and vice presidential candidates representing minor parties if Section 315 were suspended than they do when it is operative.

Suspending Section 315 (a) of the Communications Act would give broadcasters more control than they now have over access of candidates to the electorate. Control could simply shift from one private group (present large contributors) to another (individual

36. *Equal Time*, Hearings, p. 257.

FIGURE 10. Free Time Provided Presidential Candidates of Minor Parties Compared with Time Provided All Presidential Candidates by Television and Radio Networks, General Elections, 1956–68[a]

Dark areas represent time given minor party candidates

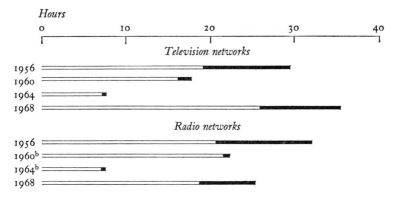

Sources: FCC, *Survey of Political Broadcasting, 1960,* Table 14; *1964,* Table 5; *1968,* Table 5. Gore Committee Report, Exhibit 24, p. 5.

a. Figures for 1956 and 1960 cover the period from Sept. 1 to general election date and could include some primary campaigns. Figures for 1968 include time for supporters.

b. Does not include FM stations programed separately from AM stations.

broadcasters). Broadcasters might fail to support equal access, as Senator John Pastore has suggested: "Certain Senators have a feeling that there could be a power structure developed, if it were left completely to the discretion or the judgment or the decision of the licensee. That they could in some way grant some preferences and some favors that could affect the result of the election."[37]

Section 315 affords considerable protection to candidates for public office. It requires that stations provide each candidate an opportunity to use its facilities equal to those rendered to his opponents. Without this protection, stations could completely block their broadcasting presentations. Candidates relying on television to reach their constituency view this prospect grimly, as the late Senator Claire Engle pointed out: "I would be very reluctant

37. *Campaign Broadcast Reform Act of 1969,* Hearings, p. 126.

to see this [broadcasting] industry get in the same position we are with the press, where we [don't] get any help at all."[38] A political consultant testified, "It seems to me particularly perilous to leave in the hands of a station owner who frequently is the owner of a newspaper in the town and a radio station and who frequently has very strong political views of his own—to leave in his hands the decision about whether or not a candidate gets time."[39] Another leading consultant commented: "I have some doubts about the wisdom of removing Section 315. I really feel that there would be some abuse. . . . It seems to me that if there are abuses when you *have* Section 315—and believe me there are more than you would ever think—then there would be just that many more without Section 315." Fear of such abuses abounds in Washington. The director of the National Committee for an Effective Congress told a U.S. Senate committee: "There are instances in which candidates find that Section 315 provides them with just about the only access they have to any form of advertising media. One such candidate told me recently of his experience with private sources. He was ignored by the newspapers as news, and refused by others, such as printers, billboard dealers, and even the newspaper ad department, as a paid customer. Had not Section 315 been a controlling factor in this situation, broadcasters might even have responded similarly. That this man won the election is proof that he was an authentic spokesman for a sizeable segment of the population, and that such problems are not always limited to just the nuisance candidate."[40] And Senator John Pastore, long an advocate of suspending Section 315, stated: "We have many members of Congress who for one reason or another have considered themselves burned at times. It may be a politician is a pretty sensitive fellow at campaign time, and that he exaggerates. Nevertheless there have been some occasions. It came up on the floor the last

38. *Political Broadcasting*, Hearings before the Senate Committee on Commerce, 87 Cong. 2 sess. (1962), p. 71.
39. *Campaign Broadcast Reform Act of 1969*, Hearings, p. 153.
40. *Ibid.*, p. 53.

time we amended 315, and there were certain strong statements made by certain Senators who had had sorrowful experiences."[41]

Suspending Section 315(a) could also enable broadcasters to make their offers of free time contingent on acceptance of their format—which could limit the candidate's ability to appear before the electorate in the way he believed to be most effective. Witness the following colloquy at a Senate hearing considering suspending Section 315:

> SENATOR MONRONEY: Your bill also would give permanently the right to the broadcaster to have whatever type of program he wished, would it not?
>
> The broadcasters would tell you whether you had to debate your opponent, they would tell you whether you had to have a press conference.
>
> SENATOR HARTKE: Oh, no.
>
> SENATOR MONRONEY: Yes, it would. If we suspend equal time, they will be in full charge without any choice, except that you can stay off and then they can say we have an empty chair here of the other candidate.[42]

A political consultant commented: "I don't believe that we should leave it to the station to determine how a candidate will present himself. Exposure is what is important. And it is too important to be left to someone like Julian Goodman [president of NBC]." Given the effectiveness of television in reaching voters, an industry-imposed format could influence the sorts of candidates nominated for office. A candidate's ability to exploit a given format may be irrelevant to his likely performance in office. But industry-preferred formats are no less relevant than those that candidates choose.

One difficulty of the present finance system is the obligations it imposes on candidates to contributors who may later desire policy-oriented favors. Public policy encouraging broadcasters to grant free time (or other services, such as voluntary advertising rate discounts) to candidates could afford the industry a means of dis-

41. *Ibid.*, p. 126.
42. *Equal Time*, Hearings, p. 47.

tributing favors. Since broadcasting is a government regulated industry, candidates, when elected, could influence the regulation of their recent benefactors. Services granted voluntarily to candidates could impose obligations upon officeholders to vote for the interests of stations that have granted expensive benefits. Stimson Bullitt, a Seattle, Washington, broadcaster who favors government-imposed requirements for this reason, criticized a reform plan containing a voluntary service component before a U.S. Senate subcommittee: "It seems to me it smacks of the railroad passes, which caused some impairment of the quality of public life a half century ago, where things are handed out free by the regulated to the regulators."[43] A station manager commented: "But the larger issue here is that we should keep our relationship with politicians at arm's length. We don't want to get into bed with them. Yet anything that is done in this area will tend in that direction."

None of these objections to suspending Section 315(a) of the Communications Act poses insurmountable difficulties. Suspension could be limited to presidential candidates and the protections of the equal time clause be retained for those seeking lesser offices. Format control may create an inconvenience for candidates and their media consultants, but the information produced by these formats may provide information to the electorate of a higher quality than that available now. Assuring minor party candidates some access to the airwaves could be a part of any suspension of equal time requirements for the presidency. The FCC has proposed, for example, that stations granting major party candidates facilities be required to do the same for candidates of "significant" minor parties (but not for fringe candidates).[44] It should not be difficult to define "significant" minor party candidates in such a way as to assure that any candidate who has a chance of winning electoral votes would have access to free time equal to that of major party candidates.

43. *Campaign Broadcast Reform Act of 1969*, Hearings, p. 130.
44. See *ibid.*, pp. 74–76.

Conclusion

The chief aims of campaign finance reform are to increase the opportunity for citizens to gather information about candidates and to equalize the ability of candidates to disseminate their messages. These are rather idealistic goals. Many citizens do not care to hear more about candidates. Even if they do, many of the messages they hear are only marginally educational. Change would not alter these basic facts. Neither can the struggle for office ever be equalized. Even if two candidates have the same amount of television time, for example, the better financed can buy expensive production techniques that may make his presentations more effective. Despite the idealism of these goals, and their obviously unrealistic bases, they have merit. If changes permitted candidates time or money to make their case, perhaps the contests would become more nearly equal than they are now. Perhaps the underfinanced candidate could make his case somewhat more easily. Concomitantly, perhaps the general public could see or hear (even in marginally educational messages) a clearer presentation of the alternatives confronting them. Achievement of even a small part of these idealistic aims would be no mean accomplishment.

The better part of the reformers' "public participation" argument, however, lies in another direction. They propose to make candidates and officeholders less dependent upon financial backers, which would have far-reaching consequences. It might well alter the positions they take both as candidates and as officeholders. It would provide them a means to make a minimal campaign even if big backers refused to contribute. Reform would thus diminish the gatekeeper role of the big donor. If change produced some small movement in the direction of greater voter choice, this too would be no small accomplishment.

☆

Chapter Five

☆

WHO SAVES
AND WHO PAYS?

THE CHIEF AIM of most reform proposals is maximizing participation, a goal that few can fault. But achieving this goal sooner or later requires money, which does produce conflict. All reform plans, whether they be the ones Congress has approved in the past or those likely to be proposed in the future, shift at least some of the costs of campaigning from candidates and party organizations to others. These cost shifts must consequently be a part of any evaluation of finance reform. Opponents, for example, often emphasize the monetary impact of the reform proposals they oppose. They sometimes assert that political parties could raise necessary funds if they were more energetic, that broadcasting plans may reduce costs negligibly and could increase them, that service plans will not provide benefits to all candidates who need them, or that reform plans discriminate against the television and radio industry.

Parties as Fund Raisers

There are those who believe that present campaign financing difficulties could be solved if political parties pursued contributors more energetically. One veteran party official, for example, commented: "You can raise funds in this country for almost anything just by asking. The trouble with political parties is that they just haven't asked. They're too lazy." He represents a group that believes that political parties are capable of doing more to solve their financial problems. Herbert Alexander has stated, "To be perfectly frank, the Democratic Party at the national level has not tried as hard as the Republican Party to raise money in small sums."[1] And Alexander Heard once testified, "My point is simply that I believe that the parties can do some of the things that need to be done themselves, by improving the effectiveness of their own fund raising operations."[2]

Supporters of finance change argue that the present performance of political parties vividly demonstrates that they cannot consistently raise enough money from small contributors to finance high cost campaigns. Most of the respondents interviewed for this study agree. Democratic party officials, for example, generally regret their party's poor performance in pursuing contributors in recent years. Republicans have been more successful in raising money, and some of them argue that parties could handle the financing problem if they would—but even many of them agree that raising campaign funds is a more formidable task than parties have been able to undertake. One party official indicated that he believed that parties could finance their nonelection year operations but could not raise enough from small contributors to finance campaigns. And a Republican senator commented: "I think that it's unfair to say that parties have not been energetic enough in raising money. The simple fact of the matter is that it is impossible to raise the large amounts of money that are necessary for campaigning, in the short amount of time you have for doing it, through small contributions. So when you are faced with the problem, with the necessity, of raising these large amounts, you turn to the large

1. *Political Campaign Financing Proposals*, Hearings before the Senate Committee on Finance, 90 Cong. 1 sess. (1967), p. 350. Alexander argues in *Responsibility in Party Finance* (Princeton, N.J.: Citizens' Research Foundation, 1963) that parties in general must assume more responsibility for developing new methods and structures for raising money. He does not discount the obstacles for attaining this goal, however (see especially pp. 20–30).

2. *1956 Campaign Contributions and Practices*, Hearings before the Senate Committee on Rules and Administration, 84 Cong. 2 sess. (1956), p. 78.

contributors. You do it every time. So where does it leave you? We have to do something, and you can't argue against the necessity of doing it by suggesting that it is possible for parties to raise the necessary money in small sums."

Political parties, after ample opportunity to demonstrate their ability, have failed their fund-raising task. They have not vigorously pursued donors. Nor have they built broad based financial support for campaigns. Solution of finance problems in the future must not rely totally upon a mechanism that has failed in the past.

Service versus Cash Benefits

Direct monetary subsidies have two advantages over plans providing services such as broadcast time and mailing privileges to candidates. Money can be universally deployed, so that a candidate can buy the services that best fit the needs of his district and his own style of campaigning. By contrast, service plans may provide products that the candidate employs either inefficiently or not at all. Campaign requirements vary by office, candidate, and district. Some office seekers use newspaper advertising and billboard displays to win votes. Others emphasize voter-registration drives and election-day services. Many count on television to generate voter interest. But some candidates live in districts where television is not useful: there may be no stations in the district, or time costs in a large metropolitan area, even at reduced rates, may be prohibitive. In these cases, television service plans may neither increase candidate-voter access nor reduce costs. Supplying services could encourage a candidate to use those he ordinarily finds useless. Since most proposals require the candidate to share in the cost of the services, these plans could drive up campaign costs.

A congressman, explaining his opposition to a bill that would provide candidates reduced-cost television and radio time, commented: "Philosophically, it is not equitable. There are many candidates who wouldn't be helped by it—who couldn't take advantage of its provisions. So the fact that it is not generally applicable weighs heavily against it."

Cash benefit plans have the advantage of providing more comprehensive relief than service plans. Both the Presidential Campaign Fund Act of 1966 and the Revenue Act of 1971, for example, made money available to finance a variety of activities. Most service plans, by contrast, provide a single service, usually broadcast time or mailing privileges. They offer only partial solutions, and, if adopted, may dissipate the energy of reformers who might otherwise work for more comprehensive reform.

But it is usually easier to generate support for service than for money proposals. Money requires direct appropriations and Congress often more willingly votes indirect subsidies, with a less visible bite on the federal treasury (broadcast rate discounts, of course, require no government money). Money's transferability increases its potency, and its possibly unpalatable consequences. Officials fear that party wheelhorses could use public subsidies to finance primary election opponents, to entrench themselves in office, or to shore up the power of a party faction. Services, by contrast, tend to be nontransferable and tied directly to candidates. Service plans may also be easier than cash benefit plans to justify as in the broad public interest—voter education (television and mailing privileges), good citizenship (voting registration plans), and so on. In addition, single-item service plans may attract support from those who are willing to try piecemeal changes but are opposed to direct subsidy proposals that usually aim at more comprehensive reform.

Both service and cash benefit plans have advantages and disadvantages. It is easier, however, to strike a good compromise with service plans than with cash benefit plans. By tying several service plans together in one package, their benefits can be made more comprehensive and usable by more candidates.

The Diversion Problem

The diversion of money saved by service benefits to other campaign expenses is an especial difficulty of all service reform proposals. Uncertainty writ large is characteristic of campaigns, and this inflates their costs. As one senator put it, "I could always use more." And a veteran of several presidential campaigns commented: "No matter how much you save on television, it will not represent a net savings unless you prohibit certain kinds of expenditures. The reason for this is simple. You can always use every last dime you get. Mailings are important. So are election day expenses, travel, advance-operations, and so on." There is a distinct possibility, then, that candidates and their managers would divert any money saved by broadcasting or other service proposals into other campaign expenses.

Opponents of such broadcast service plans as the rate discount requirement in the 1970 reform act contend that services for which candidates must bear partial cost might actually increase, rather than reduce, costs. Economic considerations presently preclude the use of television in some congressional districts. Large urban area stations with large audiences charge premium rates for time. Their broadcast signal may cover dozens of congressional districts, and candidates desiring to reach their district may have to buy an audience several times the size of the one they mean to reach. High charges coupled with wasted audiences mitigate against these candidates using television. Rate discounts (either voluntary or required), by reducing these advertising diseconomies, could encourage candidates not presently using television to do so. A network executive explained: "In many instances television is not used in [congressional] campaigns now because it is too inefficient. But with these discounts available, opponents are going to step in and start using it. Once one does, the incumbent will have to also. So they will find total outlays to be higher than they would otherwise be."

Plans that provide for reduced costs in the general election may also tempt candidates to push up expenditures during primaries. As general election costs go down, the nomination becomes more attractive, and candidates may be willing to spend more in the primaries to get it. Moreover, office seekers might divert money to the primaries that they will not have to save to use in the general election. General election savings might not compensate for higher primary costs, and total campaign expenses may thus increase.

Service plans, then, do raise the possibility that candidates will divert money that is saved to other expenses. The problem can be averted by providing the candidate benefits for a variety of services. The more services he receives, the less likely he will be to take money saved on one and spend on another. Also, spending limitations can be set for items within the campaign budget. The 1970 reform bill, for example, contained spending limitations for broadcast time in part to keep candidates from spending money saved by rate discounts for more broadcast time. The 1971 bill applied the prohibition to other advertising media as well.

Will Broadcast Service Plans Reduce Costs?

Reform plans, to operate successfully, should reduce the amount candidates must spend to wage their campaign. The few precedents available permit no decisive conclusions; but several observations suggest that broadcasting rate reductions would at least stabilize and probably decrease campaign costs, despite the problem of diverted expenditures.

The assurance of assistance might reduce the pressure on the candidate and his organization to raise funds. A U.S. senator states: "I imagine that if I knew I had so much television time that it would take the heat off me. I wouldn't worry quite so much about raising money, or feel that I had to raise it. That's what I think. I don't know what would happen in a real campaign." Most office seekers prepare campaign budgets that they attempt to adhere to. If they could build into their budgets the guaranteed assistance, they could lower the amount they would have to seek from other sources. Since many candidates do not like to solicit funds, they might avoid asking for contributions, particularly from sources they would rather shun.

Candidates' fear of overexposure also could serve as a restraint. A media consultant commented, "There are limits to the effectiveness that you can have with television." Though money saved on broadcast time might go to other campaign items, their relatively lower costs might lead to reduced overall campaign costs.

Broadcast service plans might also cause contributors to believe that candidates no longer needed their money and to cease contributing. As a political consultant put it, "If plans were adopted which gave free television time I think that the money freed by this would be used for other matters—if it were available. But [passing these plans] would seriously affect your ability to raise money. A good number of people who now give would say that we didn't need their money now since television, a most costly item, was provided free of charge." The candidate, deserted by his supporters, might have no other choice but to decrease expenditures.

Both voluntary and required rate discounts have been advocated by those who wish to reduce total campaign costs. While both have shortcomings, voluntary discounts can never be as comprehensive as required rate discounts. Stations offering voluntary reductions usually operate in large, lucrative metropolitan areas— New York, Chicago, Philadelphia, Los Angeles, and so on. Few stations located in small, less lucrative markets have volunteered discounts, and they are unlikely to do so. Some depend upon political advertising to turn a profit. Others operate on a very narrow profit margin. Candidates contesting for offices in many areas thus will not encounter voluntary discounts; such discounts will never be as potent as required reductions in reducing campaign costs for a large number of office seekers.

Those who advocate suspending Section 315's equal time rule advance increasing participation in the electoral process as a primary goal rather than saving candidates money. The presidential election of 1960 may, however, provide a guide to the possible cost savings of suspending Section 315 (a). Presidential spending for broadcast time is available for only 1956 and 1968 (Table 1). But general election expenditures for network time (which few other than presidential candidates bother to buy) are almost the same for those years (Table 2). It seems reasonable to assume that nearly all network expenditures in 1960 and 1964 as well were made by presidential candidates.

The general election network expenditures indicate that presidential candidates spent less for broadcast time in 1960 than in 1956. Although television network spending decreased only slightly, the suspension apparently permitted presidential candidates to hold the line on expenditures in 1960; in the next election their network spending had grown by 30 percent and between 1964 and 1968 it grew by 93 percent. Presidential spending for radio network time declined dramatically—by 75 percent—between 1956 and 1960. The 1960 equal time suspension probably made a greater impact on radio than on television network spending because of differences in emphasis in their spending. In 1956, presidential candidates spent 95.2 percent of their radio network budgets on program time, but only 84.6 percent of their television network budgets for programs.[3] It is likely that the modern trend toward spots developed first on television. Since radio network spending plans for 1960 probably still concentrated heavily on programs, and since the 1960 debates more likely substituted for program than for spot time, radio spending fell much more than television.

Since 1960, presidential spending for broadcasting has grown at appreciable rates even though broadcasters have granted candidates increasing amounts of free time in programing that is presently exempt from Section 315(a) requirements (Figure 7). The kind of free time offered may thus make the crucial difference in candidate spending for broadcast time. The 1960 suspension, in contrast to other years, made it possible for networks to offer explicit amounts of time, in advance of campaign planning, to

3. See *1956 General Election Campaigns*, Report of the Subcommittee on Privileges and Elections to the Senate Committee on Rules and Administration, 85 Cong. 1 sess. (1957), Exhibit 24, p. 4.

major candidates, and these office seekers were able to plan and budget accordingly. The debate format, moreover, concentrated the impact of each candidate's message and attracted large audiences—both priceless commodities that would have been difficult to duplicate. Free time programing in 1960 thus substituted for normal campaign programing. In other years it did not because candidates could not count on specified amounts of time in advance and the audiences attracted were often marginal.

Again, the increasing emphasis on spots may account for rising expenditures. Between 1956 and 1968, presidential allocation for spots on television networks increased from 15.4 percent to 47.8 percent, on radio networks from 4.8 percent to 68.2 percent.[4] The increased emphasis on spots for radio probably accounts for the greater rate of increase in radio network spending than in television spending since that time. Free time offerings, like debates, usually substitute for program length time, not the spot time that candidates have increasingly preferred. Presidential candidates have consequently increased their spending for television and radio network time despite the availability of growing amounts of commercially sponsored free time on these networks. They could, of course, have spent even more if the free time had not been available. It is possible, however, that had debates—which can attract even larger audiences than spots provide—been made a part of the free time offerings, the emphasis on spots would have diminished.

The 1960 suspension of Section 315(a) did enable presidential candidates to temporarily stabilize broadcasting expenditures. Despite this, total costs for presidential campaigns rose as fast (or faster) between 1956 and 1960 as they did in other years (see Figure 1). This could indicate that 1960 broadcast savings were diverted to other items. But total costs might have increased even more had the suspension not been in effect. It is thus impossible to calculate the impact of the 1960 suspension or any future suspension on total presidential campaign costs.

4. See *ibid.*, and Federal Communications Commission, *Survey of Political Broadcasting, 1968*, Table 5.

Who Pays?

All plans designed to neutralize the force of campaign funding must specify where the money is to come from. Generally, some combination of government, private individual, and industry sources is designated. Tax incentive proposals, for example, envision creating new sources of funds whose ultimate cost would be borne by both government and private individuals. The 1966 and 1971 tax check-off proposals rely entirely on government money while various free time proposals place the cost burden on broadcasters. Other plans contemplate joint industry-government financing. The Twentieth Century Fund's Voters' Time plan requires the government to pay for the cost of the time provided candidates on broadcasting facilities and stations to charge for the time at a discount. Others shift the burden even further to private industry. The 1970 reform bill passed by Congress required broadcasters to give advertising rate discounts, and the 1971 plan in effect reduced charges of a broader group of advertisers.

IMPOSING REQUIREMENTS ON BROADCASTERS

The industry most often singled out to provide services (or money) is broadcasting. Broadcast expenses currently occupy a preeminent place in the budgets of candidates contesting statewide and national office. Broadcast services could thus offer substantial assistance to a large number of office seekers. Television's visibility also makes the need for this service more dramatic than for other services. Broadcast service plans, moreover, do not require direct appropriations from the federal treasury. Mandatory rate reductions do not even require indirect federal subsidies, unless stations are allowed to make an equivalent reduction from their taxable income.

Justifying requirements on broadcasters. Broadcasting occupies a unique niche in this country. Its unsurpassed power to reach large audiences gives it an unusual public character. It is a private industry but the physical property of its operation, the airwaves, is a scarce public resource. As a Senate Commerce Committee study explains, "the airwaves belong to the public. The physical phenomenon accommodating the broadcast spectrum is a Government resource. Some industries subjected to Government regulation could carry on their basic function without regulation. Broadcasting, as it is known today, cannot exist otherwise."[5]

Broadcasters cannot function without government regulation because their transmission signals would interfere with each other, as they did prior to regulation, making it impossible for audiences to receive clear signals. Other regulated industries, by contrast, could continue to operate without government direction: interstate movers to move, telephone companies to connect callers (even long distance calls could be transmitted without the use of microwave signals, although at additional expense), power companies to sell power. The rationale of most utility regulation is that the large capital outlay required to provide services makes competition in a local setting impossible (in the case of telephones, subscribing to several companies serving a single community would also be inconvenient). The economies of scale presumably accrue to the consumer, who pays less for the utility's services than he otherwise would.

As a condition for granting utilities a franchise to operate, the government could presumably require them to provide services to candidates in return. Consumers, however, pay directly (rather than indirectly as for broadcasting) for the services of utilities. These companies could consequently pass the cost of lost revenue to the consumer, a prospect that would generate little support among the public.

Government agencies do not regulate newspapers and magazines, the two major journalistic and advertising competitors of broadcasting. But they have provided them special mailing rates that permit more rapid distribution of their product at less cost

5. *Fairness Doctrine*, a staff report prepared for the Senate Committee on Commerce, 90 Cong. 2 sess. (1968), p. 114.

than other mailers bear. This amounts to a government subsidy. Magazines, the bulk of which are distributed by mail, would be especially hard hit without this subsidy. Even without tapping public moneys, however, newspapers and magazines could continue printing, if they could survive economically. The First Amendment of the U.S. Constitution, moreover, guarantees freedom of the press. Although this freedom applies to both the printed and the electronic press, it has thus far served as a more effective barrier to permanent government incursions for the former than for the latter.

Broadcasting's unique position is the principal reason reformers single it out to provide free or reduced cost time to candidates. Since broadcasters operate through government largess which grants them a license to exploit the scarce airwaves for private benefit, the government can exact whatever it wishes in return for the right to use these airwaves, or as former Senator Albert Gore said: "The public owns the airwaves which we give the television and radio stations permission to use, and the license to use. It is a very profitable license. And as a condition of that license, we could reserve a certain percentage of time for civic purposes."[6] Broadcasting is also more visible to the public than are other regulated or subsidized industries. Few know, for example, that telephone companies use airwaves in long-distance microwave transmissions, nor does everyone understand the mail subsidy that supports magazine distribution. But many people do know that broadcasters depend upon the airwaves to transmit their signals, that the public owns these airwaves, and that the public therefore has the right to require something from broadcasters in return for this benefit. Television is, of course, far more important to campaigning than are other regulated or subsidized industries. Broadcast costs reach a magnitude unmatched by airline or railroad travel, telephone communications, or newspaper and magazine advertising. Television's ability to reach large numbers of voters

6. *Political Campaign Financing Proposals*, Hearings, p. 130.

with messages that dramatically affect their behavior surpasses that of the printed media. These reasons provide justification for singling out broadcasters to provide campaign services.

The reaction of broadcasters. Most broadcasters are hostile to proposals requiring them to provide free or reduced cost services to candidates (see pages 65–69). No industry views placidly the prospect of government regulation that affects business practices central to its economy. And broadcasters see no comparable requirements being placed on competitors for the advertising dollar.

Various voluntary proposals have been submitted by broadcasters to meet demands for the relief of mounting campaign costs. Some stations have offered advertising rate reductions. Certain segments of the industry support suspending or modifying Section 315(a) of the Communications Act, which could encourage stations to voluntarily grant more free time to candidates. Advocates of voluntary plans believe their proposals would permit them maximum flexibility to meet needs for broadcast time without placing undue burdens on stations. Some broadcasters fear that mandatory plans would impose economic hardships on them. Many television stations, for example, do not produce profits; in 1968, 130 of the 570 stations reporting profits and losses to the Federal Communications Commission suffered losses.[7] Requirements that stations provide candidates free or reduced cost time could drive some out of business and turn others into money losers. Voluntary reductions would be less catastrophic because stations would have maximum freedom in scheduling programs and commercials—both vital to a station's economic productivity. Voluntary service plans would also permit stations maximum flexibility in responding to specific local needs in covering candidates. Broadcasters argue that their interpretation of local needs should prove considerably more equitable than the formulas of a far-away bureaucracy that must be applied in disparate circumstances throughout the country.

Reactions to broadcasters' charges. Some advocates of mandatory

7. Federal Communications Commission, *35th Annual Report/Fiscal Year 1969*, p. 136.

broadcasting service plans respond to charges that their proposals discriminate against broadcasters by suggesting that all regulated or subsidized industries be required to provide services. As a party finance official put it: "It is not an argument against television rate reductions. It's really an argument for including other federally regulated industries." Others would discard the public airwaves argument completely, obviating the necessity of explaining the imposition of requirements on one regulated industry but not another. As explained by an adviser to several presidential candidates: "If you're going to hit television alone, do it frankly. We single them out because they now represent the most important expenditure in most campaigns. . . . This is really all the justification you need."

Conclusion

The paucity of experience with plans providing financial relief to candidates for public office makes it difficult to gauge the precise impact of reform on the cost of campaigning. Even failure to produce savings, however, should not be reason to discard attempts at reform. The primary fault of private campaign financing is not high costs but the way in which money must be raised (and the consequences of this for the electoral process and public policy making). If reform reduced office seekers' dependence upon wealthy contributors, it would produce worthy results even though it produced no net total savings. The public participation arguments are more compelling reasons for finance reform than is any speculation that finance changes will reduce campaign expenditures.

☆

Chapter Six

☆

PROBLEMS OF ADMINISTRATION

THE ADMINISTRATIVE difficulties entailed in changes have always plagued finance reform. In the past, the advocates of change divided over their preferred approaches. Opponents frequently exploited their differences. Future difficulties, as Congress experiments with change (by actually approving reform bills), will center on questions about the impact and direction of reform. The most important of the potential administrative problems involve which candidates are eligible, what elections are covered, and (in a broadcast service plan) how format is controlled and how stations are to meet candidates' time demands. Other, equally serious administrative problems focus on broadcasters' voluntary actions to provide free time or reduce charges.

Which Candidates to Aid

Should reform proposals provide help only to presidential candidates or include other candidates? The greatest number propose assisting presidential (and vice presidential) candidates. Others include U.S. senators and representatives, and some add state governors. Only a few cover candidates for all elective offices, estimated to number over 500,000.[1]

The case for including only the presidency is strong. The glam-

1. See U.S. Bureau of the Census, *1967 Census of Governments*, Vol. 6, No. 1, p. 1.

our, visibility, importance, and high campaign cost of the office make it easy to dramatize campaign finance problems, and thus to build public support for change. Congress may be more willing to vote benefits to candidates for offices other than their own, particularly that of president. Members of Congress do not wish to encourage opposition for their seats or to give up their advantages of incumbency by providing compensating advantages to potential opponents. The single, presidential contest generates far fewer administrative headaches than would a plan covering 536 offices (the presidency plus senators and representatives) or 500,000 (all elected officials).

The case for including other offices is also strong, for campaign finance problems are more intense for lesser offices than for the presidency. Presidential candidates can attract funds more readily than can other candidates, as Senator Strom Thurmond, who has contested for the presidency as well as other offices, has observed: "I think that it is easier to attract financing for the top job in the Nation than it is for any of the lesser jobs. Second, a contribution of $1,000 or more has a much greater weight in terms of the influence it may buy if it is contributed in a congressional race than it would be in a presidential race."[2] Presidential candidates who fail to attract adequate funds have more resources to compensate for this failure than do those contesting lesser offices. A labor union political activist commented: "You could make the argument that it would be better to do something for [candidates other than the presidency] at the federal level. After all, a president can get news coverage. He can often get his message across by other means. But a congressional candidate can't." Finally, the presidency's greater visibility makes it easier to prevent campaign finance abuse there than elsewhere. Large contributors may be more able to influence the activities of lesser officials, who undergo less intense public scrutiny (usually through the press) than does the president.

2. *Political Campaign Financing Proposals*, Hearings before the Senate Committee on Finance, 90 Cong. 1 sess. (1967), p. 424.

Each approach is compelling. The difficulty of reconciling them has delayed campaign finance reform. As if this were not enough, another question of eligibility compounds this problem. Assuming the problem of which offices to assist is resolved, the next question is which candidates contesting the eligible offices qualify for assistance.

A dozen or more candidates regularly contest presidential elections, most of them polling a tiny fraction of 1 percent of the vote. More than two candidates vie for many Senate and House seats. Should finance reform provide all comers the same benefits regardless of their likely strength at the polls? If all candidates do not qualify for assistance, where should the line be drawn? Granting assistance to all office seekers may proliferate candidacies. It certainly penalizes major party nominees, who poll the bulk of the votes, by denying them benefits proportionate to their vote-getting power. On the other hand, plans that exclude minor candidates restrict the competition of ideas and may block the way to policy change.

The largest number of reform proposals dealing with eligibility problems have provided aid only to presidential candidates or at most to candidates for all federal offices. Most of the proposals have originated at the national level, where action focuses more readily on national than state offices. Senator Russell Long has noted the benefits that help for presidential candidates could bring to candidates for other offices: "If I do say it, one good thing about this measure, if we get it into effect, is that it will keep the President and Vice President from coming through and just hauling all the money the Democrats can find out of our States and leave something there for the candidate for Congress and the Senate to solicit rather than the whole place having been harvested by the presidential candidates."[3]

Reform plans that designate which offices are eligible usually specify also which candidates within those offices qualify for

3. *Ibid.*, p. 135.

assistance. In general, plans that call for the federal government to provide money or services have limited assistance to candidates representing the two major parties. Some have also provided benefits to candidates of "significant" minor parties, usually defined as those polling a certain percentage of votes in the previous election. Rate discount plans, tax incentives, and others not requiring direct government spending (except the suspension of Section 315[a] of the Communications Act) have generally been available to all candidates contesting the eligible offices.

Which Elections to Cover

Many states require primaries, where party nominees are chosen in public elections. Since nomination is essential to the contest for office, the primary is the first and crucial step toward election. In areas where one party dominates, winners of the primary invariably win the general election. Because of primaries' obvious importance, some proponents of campaign finance reform have protested against legislation that does not cover them: "In many communities the primary election is the election. So, it seems to me it should be included."[4] David Adamany, a student of campaign finance, stated, "From the candidate's perspective, money may be more important in the nominating process than in the general election. In primaries there is no party label voting [no means of distinguishing one candidate for an office from another because of party label] and less early voter decision; the electorate is more easily influenced by the kinds of campaigning that money can buy."[5]

But the case for excluding primaries from reform proposals appears even stronger than that for including them. Reform at the general election level would remove many of the deficiencies that cause the electoral process to fall short of the requirements of

4. Representative Charles Vanik, in *The Campaign Broadcast Reform Act of 1969*; Hearings before the Senate Committee on Commerce, 91 Cong. 1 sess. (1969), p. 142.
5. *Financing Politics* (University of Wisconsin Press, 1969), p. 268.

democratic theory. It could, for example, promote vigorous and effective competition in the final election. And it would reduce the premium presently placed on candidates who either have their own money or can raise it when nominations are being made. When more aid is available for general election contestants, there may be less reason to assist primary election candidates. The promotion of a vigorous competition (for example, by insuring equal or minimum access of major contesters to the voters) may be a higher order requirement of democratic theory than a mere escalation in the number of candidates who contest for office, which seems to be a chief goal of supplying assistance at the primary level.

There is no reason, moreover, for believing that money is more important in primaries than in general elections. One of the most intensive studies of primary campaigns (which may have relevance for other primary contests) concluded that monetary resources were no more likely to explain primary than general election victories; it generally discounted any differences in the impact of money on the two elections.[6] Several administrative difficulties militate against inclusion of primaries in reform proposals: Numerous candidates frequently contest primary nominations; as many as a half dozen is common; often there are more. Unless all comers are to receive assistance, some system must be devised for determining who is and is not a serious candidate. Providing benefits to all could so increase the number of candidates as to make voters' choice more difficult. It could also prove to be very costly. The wide divergence in primary laws from state to state also creates a problem of designing a law that would provide comparable benefits throughout the country.

Which Format to Subsidize

Finance plans that advance free or reduced cost broadcasting time can specify the format that candidates must use to take ad-

6. See William Buchanan and Agnes Bird, *Money as a Campaign Resource: Tennessee Democratic Senatorial Primaries, 1948–1964* (Princeton, N.J.: Citizens' Research Foundation, 1966), pp. 84–89.

vantage of the time. A key question is whether they should provide spot time benefits to candidates.

Those who oppose them argue that spots communicate little information and may distort a candidate's image and record. A Federal Communications Commissioner commented: "It is impossible to get at the issue in a short 30 second or 60 second spot. It takes at least five minutes. And they can be very misleading." "You can't really say anything in 30 seconds," according to one congressman. "About all that you can do is identify yourself and make some minor appeal." It is also possible that slick Madison Avenue advertising techniques can fabricate an image of a candidate that can then be huckstered to the American people in much the same way as a bar of soap.[7] Those who resist including spots in reduced-cost broadcasting plans assert that government-directed change should encourage formats providing longer time segments that assure more comprehensive and conscientious discussion of the issues.

The supporters of spot time benefits offer candidates' increased use of spots as a primary reason for including it. "This is what candidates are using," one congressional staffer explained. "Therefore, if we want to be helpful we have to hit this area." Spots also provide many voters their only exposure to candidates; longer programs frequently attract only the party faithful. Candidates thus capitalize on spots to reach large uncommitted audiences and to capture the average television viewer (and voter) whose attention span is short. Proponents of spot time maintain that its inclusion is necessary if the two primary goals of finance change—saving candidates money and guaranteeing them a minimum access to voters—are to be achieved.

A number of advocates of spot time benefits argue that high-quality information can be transmitted in political commercials. The president of an advertising firm testified before a U.S. Senate subcommittee: "I think that [spots] are informative. . . . I think

7. This is one of the primary points advanced by Joe McGinnis, *The Selling of the President 1968* (Trident, 1969).

that they tend to illuminate issues, they are constructive. I think they are good for the electorate."[8] A leading media consultant commented, "Just because you communicate in pragmatic terms is no sign that you have communicated useful information. We have seen for example in several elections—Nixon, Johnson, Kennedy, Roosevelt—that what the candidate actually says about issues makes little difference once he is in office. So who is to say that [this] provides information that is more relevant than that which tells what kind of person a candidate is, how he acts toward other human beings, and this sort of thing?" He added, "Time is not the relevant factor in determining what can be communicated in nonlinear transmission." One media consultant, contending that commercials do not mislead (even if their producers intend otherwise), commented: "I think that the American people are not going to be fooled. If you are inauthentic in the small commercials, they are going to see through it." Nor do longer programs guarantee more honest or authentic presentations than spots. Candidates can present contrived performances on longer programs also, particularly when they have control of the format.

The differing goals of reformers add to the controversy: some emphasize saving money, others seek to guarantee candidate-voter access. The latter stress the educational value of broadcast time and the duty to use public money to promote voter education rather than for the convenience of candidates. Advocates of cost savings, on the other hand, prefer spot time because candidates use it, and assistance for services ought to go where candidates use it.

Various reform proposals have handled the allocation of time differently. The Twentieth Century Fund's Voters' Time proposal provides assistance for program time only. A proposal by the National Committee for an Effective Congress, however, presents an alternative that may be the solution to the conflict over spot time. It requires rate reductions for both spot and program length time.[9] Reductions for spots could help candidates save money and

8. *Campaign Broadcast Reform Act of 1969*, Hearings, p. 153.
9. See *ibid.*, pp. 1-3.

reach large groups of voters—with a message that may or may not be educational. Reductions for program length time encourage its use and might produce more educational messages for the smaller group of voters interested in them. Such a plan might elicit support from backers of both types of time.

Mandatory versus Voluntary Plans

Broadcast service plans either require stations to render services or encourage them to do so voluntarily. The latter include suspension of Section 315(a) of the Communications Act and voluntary rate discounts. The mandatory plans are those that require rate reductions for advertising time or designation of blocks of time for candidates (for which stations must pay all or part of the cost).

VOLUNTARY RATE DISCOUNTS

Voluntary discounts pose particular administrative difficulties. By their nature, they fail to provide comprehensive coverage, as noted by a party leader active in campaign finance: "We oppose the [voluntary] station reductions. They will not do the job because they are so scattered and will help such few districts. It just won't make as much impact as it should." Broadcasters who have made discount offers tend to be located in lucrative market areas. Those operating economically marginal stations are not likely to volunteer reductions. Broadcaster Stimson Bullitt noted the relationship of a station's profitability to its performance of public service: "The stations . . . vary greatly in their profitability, primarily according to the size of the market (and secondarily on the number of competitors with which a station shares it). Because the revenue curve in relation to market size rises more steeply than the cost curve, the net profit curve rises even more steeply than the revenue curve. As a result, a smalltown station may have an extremely small profit margin and a big-city one, a large margin. This variation in profitability creates an equivalent variation in capacity to do useful and expensive things in the public interest."[10]

Voluntary reductions offered by stations vary considerably, ranging from 25 to 50 percent. Even stations serving the same market often grant differing discounts. Stations with larger reductions for political advertising could find it difficult to meet the demand for time. Those with lower discounts may face intense pressure to bring their rates in line with others. Discrepancies in discounts may also encourage candidates to take advantage of discounts on stations they would ordinarily not prefer (because of market coverage or audience size). Nonuniform discounts could thus produce difficulties for both stations and candidates.

Opponents sometimes assert that voluntary reductions will not work because no administrative machinery without the sanction of law will compel those stations that have announced reductions to live up to their agreement. One congressional staffer, skeptical of a voluntary plan, stated: "You can't trust them to carry it out. The voluntary regulation of cigarette advertising has been a farce. We had one of the code guys in New York testify to us that he had been forced to give up work on this aspect of the code in April of 1968. Yet the N.A.B. [National Association of Broadcasters] testified in June of '69 that they were continuing their work. . . . I just don't believe that when it comes down to the actual [providing rate reductions] that they will deliver." A number of foes have adopted a wait-and-see attitude toward broadcasters actually furnishing time at reduced rates. Some of them believe that the station offers were primarily public relations responses to increased pressure in Congress that something must be done about rising campaign advertising costs. When that pressure subsides—and they think that it inevitably will—the public relations offers will disappear. They also judge the industry's past performance on voluntary corrections to be abysmal. Only administrative machinery with the sanction of law can enforce the reductions, and at that point, of course, they become mandatory rather than voluntary.

10. Herbert E. Alexander, Stimson Bullitt, and Hyman H. Goldin, "The High Costs of TV Campaigns," *Television Quarterly*, Vol. 5 (Winter 1966), p. 58.

Mandatory rate reductions are preferable to voluntary because they would apply to all stations and thus be more comprehensive. They would also be uniform and their integrity would be assured by law.

MANDATORY RATE REDUCTIONS

Mandatory discounts are opposed because they apply to all stations regardless of their profit situation. Those barely turning a profit and those in loss situations could be especially disadvantaged by such requirements.

Broadcasters frequently assert that candidates' demand for time would increase with reduced costs. They doubt that some stations, particularly television outlets in large metropolitan areas, could meet that demand. Spokesmen for the industry react particularly strongly against specific time requirements. A proposal advanced by the National Committee for an Effective Congress[11] specifies that each congressional and senatorial candidate must receive a certain amount of program and spot time at reduced rates (70–80 percent off the usual charge), to be divided among the stations covering a candidate's district. Broadcasters contend that this would place a heavy time (not to say economic) burden on some stations. Frank Stanton, president of CBS, testified that during the 1968 general elections it would have provided benefits to 109 Senate and House candidates in the New York City metropolitan area served by the network's owned station, WCBS-TV. If these candidates had taken advantage of their time during the evening hours, "WCBS-TV and each of the seven other New York City commercial stations would have had to provide one and a half hours of political program time and 23 minutes of political [spot] announcements each evening for 35 consecutive nights before the election."[12] Citing similar figures, NBC President Julian Goodman added, "This represents more commercial time than is available

11. See *Campaign Broadcast Reform Act of 1969*, Hearings, pp. 1–3.
12. *Ibid.*, p. 105.

in the entire prime-time period."[13] Neither calculation includes time that candidates not covered by the proposal might seek.

Proponents of specified time allocations assert that broadcasters exaggerate the magnitude of the demands likely to be made on them. Many congressional candidates would pass up the bargain rates and few would use their full time allotment. Moreover, the New York City area is an aberrant case. Its huge concentrated population provides the base for more election districts and candidates than even other metropolitan areas. Stations located elsewhere would not be forced to cope with time demands of the same magnitude.

But, network executives counterattack, no guarantee prevents candidates from claiming their allotted time, and providing this time could require drastic cuts in regular programing. Time discounts also would generate heavy demands in many areas, though none so great as in New York. Disruptions on New York stations, which attract approximately 10 percent of the national audience, might jeopardize network programing during the election period because of the New York audience loss. In addition to that loss, according to Stanton, "other stations across the country would be forced to preempt network broadcasts for local candidates under this bill at times which would differ from city to city—creating a checkerboard effect that would require each network to consider seriously whether it would make sense to operate during prime time for the five weeks preceding elections."[14]

Increased candidate demand for broadcasting time could also destroy viewing audiences. Frank Stanton, for example, stated: "It is difficult to conjecture how this flood of political programming could retain any but a fraction of prime-time audience levels. I fear that such stations would be carrying nothing but slogans and set pieces, to an audience consisting of campaign managers and candidates' relatives—and I am afraid close relatives at that."[15]

13. *Ibid.*, p. 121.
14. *Ibid.*, p. 106.
15. *Ibid.*

Adlai Stevenson, the Democratic presidential nominee in 1952 and 1956, would probably agree. In 1956, Stevenson forces one evening preempted five minutes of "I Love Lucy," one of television's most popular shows. Stevenson, testifying about "audience reaction," quoted the first telegram he received: "I like Ike; I love Lucy. Drop Dead."[16] Since most viewers do not prefer political programming, greater candidate use could so oversaturate broadcasting time that its ability to attract audiences would be destroyed.

Required discounts portend difficulties over allocation of benefits, disputes about who can use scarce amounts of time, and enforcement of station compliance with the law. Those who oppose discounts have contended that the Federal Communications Commission is ill equipped to handle the administrative tangle such discount plans could produce. A network executive testified that "the mind boggles at the thought of the FCC attempting to adjust the schedules of 1,000 or more candidates for 435 House seats and a third of the Senate at the same time. Among the scheduling conflicts the FCC would have to arbitrate would be conflicts between senatorial and congressional candidates in the same areas."[17]

Despite the problems associated with required rate discounts, the case for them appears strong. Their harshest difficulties can be avoided if only the discount rate, not the amount of time, is specified. Stations might of course refuse to sell time at all. But if they are required to provide some time at reduced rates, they would still have freedom to set a maximum and allocate the time they would sell among eligible candidates in accordance with other demands for time. If the mandatory discount approach incorporates some flexibility, it could avoid the pitfalls of past proposals.

SUSPENDING SECTION 315(A)

Broadcasting's most visible Washington spokesmen—the networks and the National Association of Broadcasters—advocate

16. See *Political Campaign Financing Proposals*, Hearings, p. 491.
17. *Campaign Broadcast Reform Act of 1969*, Hearings, p. 106.

suspending Section 315's equal time rule. But many broadcasters prefer to leave it as it is. An extensive survey in 1966 of broadcasters' attitudes toward changing Section 315 had the following responses:[18]

Response	Commercial radio stations		Commercial television stations	
	Number	Percent of total	Number	Percent of total
Okay as is	1,906	42.5	161	29.6
Modify	908	20.3	174	32.0
Repeal	881	19.7	154	28.3
No opinion or no answer	787	17.5	55	10.1

Overall, about as many broadcasters favored keeping Section 315 as it is as preferred to modify or repeal it. In 1970 in a survey of television station general managers' opinion about changing Section 315, the percentage opposing any change remained close to that in the 1966 survey but the percentage in favor of modifying or repealing it had increased:[19]

Response	Commercial television stations	
	Number	Percent of total
Leave as is	21	23.1
Modify	59	64.8
Repeal	5	5.5
No opinion or no response	6	6.6

18. *Fairness Doctrine*, a staff report prepared for the Senate Committee on Commerce, 90 Cong. 2 sess. (1968), pp. 141–360. The survey included 4,482 radio stations and 544 television stations.

19. Responses from 91 station managers to question 4 of the Brookings broadcast questionnaire (see Appendix): "Some advocate changing Section 315 of the Communications Act in order to free stations to give more time to major candidates, if the station desires to do so. What is your position on this matter?" Some respondents indicated under "Other" that they favored modifying Section 315, others that they favored repealing it.

Many broadcasters oppose changing Section 315 for fear of the administrative difficulties that might arise. A network executive explained that they know the meaning of Section 315: "They can live with it. They don't want to change it to something that will cause difficulties for them. They believe that problems might result. In this respect, the networks are willing to do more than the industry in general." Another network executive explained, "What we sometimes don't realize is that there are hundreds of races across the country. 315 helps a station pick its way through this maze." Section 315 or its equivalent has governed broadcasters' obligations to candidates for over forty years. Stations' experience with the rule coupled with the decisions and guidelines provided by the FCC have fashioned a clear, well-defined law. Former FCC Chairman William Henry once stated: "Because of its explicit standards and non-discriminatory nature, the equal opportunity provision has lent itself to effective application by broadcast licensees in the first instance, and has also greatly facilitated the Commission's task of administering and enforcing it. The Commission has, over the years, made a series of specific rulings under the definitive standards of the existing section and has given these rulings widespread public distribution. As a consequence, candidates and licensees are generally well informed of their rights and obligations under Section 315 and the number of complaints submitted to the Commission has been relatively few. Equally important, the Commission has been able to resolve such complaints as have been submitted within the time limits necessarily imposed by the election process."[20] Broadcasters who oppose changing Section 315 frequently cite its clear guidelines as a major reason for their opposition. Of the 21 television station managers who in the 1970 survey favored leaving the section as it is, 17 (81 percent) felt it provided clear guidelines about a station's responsibilities and obligations, 8 (38.1 percent) that stations would be more vulnerable to attack during campaigns without

20. *Equal Time*, Hearings before the Senate Committee on Commerce, 88 Cong. 1 sess. (1963), p. 65.

Section 315, and 7 (33.3 percent) that they would lose their ability to schedule candidates without it.[21]

If Section 315 (a) were repealed, station-candidate relationships would be governed by the fairness doctrine, which requires stations to provide a "reasonable opportunity" for airing various points of view held by responsible elements in the community on various issues which arise."[22] Unless an individual is attacked personally on the station, the broadcaster may choose to present these various points of view in any way he wishes and time does not have to be equal. The doctrine's vagueness might pose difficulties for candidates, stations, and the FCC if it were the primary rule governing station-candidate relationships. An FCC commissioner noted: "If we get a complaint under 315, we ask the stations some simple questions: Did you give time to his opponent as he has charged? Is the person complaining a legally qualified candidate? What do you intend to do about it? Those are easy to enforce. The Fairness Doctrine only requires a reasonable effort to present opposing viewpoints. It's more difficult to enforce."

Section 315 (a)'s clearly defined obligations also provide several advantages to stations. It offers them some protection from the overzealous candidate who might otherwise make unreasonable demands for time. As noted by one broadcaster: "You must remember that candidates are very sensitive during campaigns. If a station has to use its editorial judgment during that time it can lead to very abrasive relationships. As it is now he can say his hands are tied by the politicians in Washington." Broadcasters can also abuse this protection. It supplies a convenient excuse to those who do not wish to provide time. A station manager can tell the candidate that he would be glad to give (or sell) time to him, but if he did so he would have to do the same for the candidate's opponent. Some broadcasters, of course, want to maintain their free-

21. Responses to question 5 of the Brookings broadcast questionnaire (see Appendix): "Why do you favor leaving Section 315 of the Communications Act as it is? (Check as many as applicable)" One respondent indicated no opinion.

22. *Fairness Doctrine*, staff report, p. 5; for a discussion of the doctrine, see pp. 3–51, especially pp. 4–7.

dom to do just this; they thus oppose suspending Section 315. Finding it familiar and comfortable, they would rather live with it than hazard the problems that change might produce.

Section 3 -(a) also affords considerable protection to candidates. Broadc sters are not likely to abuse the right of presidential candidates to access, because of national visibility. But as former Republican National Committee Chairman William Miller observed, "when section 315's application is suspended as regards candidates for lesser offices, this task of monitoring becomes more and more difficult."[23] Russell Hemenway, director of the National Committee for an Effective Congress, told a U.S. Senate committee: "Presidential contests are unique. They engage the attention of the entire country, and are subject to the scrutiny of a national constituency which would be quick to rise at any indication of unfair treatment. Candidates in intra-state campaigns lack such protection, and by virtue of sheer numbers—468 Congressional races alone—would pose a herculean, and probably impossible task for any watchdog agency. Such candidates would inevitably be more subject to the whims of individual stations and local pressures."[24]

For these reasons Section 315(a) should for the present be suspended only for the presidential and vice presidential candidates. The national visibility of these candidates would prevent broadcasters' abuse of their new prerogatives. The small number of contestants would pose fewer administrative difficulties than would a more inclusive suspension. Congressmen, moreover, might be more willing to vote a suspension for presidential candidates than for themselves. In fact, the only suspension plans ever approved by both houses of Congress have applied only to presidential and vice presidential candidates. The results of a suspension at the presidential level could in time provide the experience necessary to judge whether benefits should be extended to additional candidates.

23. *Equal Time*, Hearings, p. 114.
24. *Campaign Broadcast Reform Act of 1969*, Hearings, p. 53.

THE SUPERIORITY OF MANDATORY PLANS

Advocates of voluntary proposals frequently contrast their administrative advantages to the headaches of mandatory proposals. Voluntary action, for example, leaves allocation problems—who, and how much he gets—to private industry, avoiding the rigid formulas of mandatory plans. Writing formulas for House of Representatives candidates that are flexible enough to account for differences in election districts, even among this relatively small number of offices, would create difficult problems. Voluntary plans would in effect remove a source of dissension that frequently disrupts would-be allies in their efforts to achieve change. They would also allow stations maximum flexibility in responding to their own needs and their interpretation of the widely varying needs of local areas. Mandatory plans would probably fail to account for these variations.

The problems associated with most voluntary broadcast service plans, however, preclude their meeting the objectives of most reform advocates. The lack of comprehensiveness and uniformity are severe disadvantages that cannot be adequately compensated. Suspending Section 315 (a) of the Communications Act is the only voluntary plan that could provide some relief from the difficulties of campaign financing. The administrative problems associated with such a suspension would be minimized if it were limited to presidential candidates.

Conclusions

The administrative difficulties posed by campaign finance reform plans are substantial problems. The inability of reformers to resolve these issues has hindered reform efforts in the past. But some recent innovations promise hope for the future. The Twentieth Century Fund's Voters' Time proposal, for example, provides a way to divide benefits between candidates representing major parties and those nominated by minor parties.

The 1970 reform bill also contained innovations that seemed to have bypassed some of these administrative difficulties. It succeeded because no direct spending from the federal treasury was required. Reforms requiring government money (or services costing money) must stipulate who is eligible, what the money may be spent for, how allocations will be made, and which elections will be covered. Plans that do not require direct government spending can be considerably more flexible on these points. In some instances the 1970 reform proposal did make choices— limiting spending for broadcasting by all candidates contesting federal office, and suspending Section 315(a) of the Communications Act for presidential candidates only. Once such proposals are enacted into law and applied in actual campaigns they will provide experience—with both the choices made and those not made. As experience accumulates, more definitive judgments about the advantages and disadvantages of various administrative alternatives can be made. The experience can be most beneficial if the reforms affect several election periods. Until some fragment of information based on the actual operation of reform plans appears, all contentions about their relative merits will be mere conjecture.

☆

Chapter Seven

☆

GUIDELINES FOR CHANGE

CONGRESS has twice enacted laws designed to infuse the election system with money. The Presidential Campaign Fund Act of 1966 was made inoperative before it took effect. The second tax check-off plan, contained in the Revenue Act of 1971, was devised to go into operation after the 1972 election year. With a sitting President who has promised to block implementation of the plan, its eventual fate remains uncertain. But it is certain that passage of the 1971 legislation sets the stage for continued debate about how to change campaign financing in this country.

Present System Has Received a Fair Trial

Private campaign financing has received a fair trial. It has not proven capable of supplying the money needed for modern campaigns. Moreover, it seriously subverts election and policy processes by providing men of wealth undue power, and by adulterating the democratic ideal of relatively equal influence among voters. Fund raising pressures create untenable strains on candidates and officeholders, who must in a growing number of cases weigh the impact of their decisions on contributors. Frequently, money needs redirect campaign energies from education to financing; and as costs increase, money's insidious power will also grow. For these reasons, the present campaign finance system needs reform. The reform could aid in (1) assuring all serious

140

candidates minimum access to voters; (2) increasing voters' knowledge of and information about alternatives, by enabling candidates to wage more effective campaigns; (3) reducing pressures on candidates to raise money, regardless of the response of large contributors; (4) decreasing candidates' obligations to donors and thereby contributors' leverage on public policy matters that affect them; (5) diminishing the impact of the monied as brokers who decide who can and cannot run for office; and (6) decreasing the advantage held by the wealthy in the quest for office.

A reform plan to achieve these goals could combine a package of services and incentives designed to increase private giving.

A Service Package

Combining several service plans into one package alleviates the chief disadvantages of the various plans. At the same time, their nontransferability, their obvious promotion of the broad public interest in campaigning, and their indirect means of aiding in campaign financing sidestep most of the pitfalls of direct subsidies.

CANDIDATE ACCESS TO BROADCASTING

Finance change should begin by facilitating candidates' access to television and radio facilities. Television, particularly, excels in its ability to reach people. Office seekers increasingly need it to transmit messages to voters. Easing candidate access to these facilities can thus facilitate minimum exposure of all serious candidates to the electorate, regardless of their financial capacities. Providing citizens with some exposure to candidates is also a public education service.

Broadcasters resent being singled out to provide time at reduced costs to candidates, to bear a disproportionate burden in providing services for campaigning. They dispute the argument that the federal government can require broadcasters to provide services in return for their use of the electromagnetic spectrum, which is in the public domain. But broadcasting's importance to campaigning permits no other choice about change.

Broadcasters believe that establishing time or rate requirements for political broadcasting creates a precedent that could later be extended to other areas. If only rate reductions are specified, and broadcasters are allowed to control scheduling of time, part of the sting of mandatory plans can be removed.

Both mandatory and voluntary plans have advantages; the following guidelines therefore incorporate elements of both, with voluntary provisions generally applying to higher office candidates.

Required discounts on time. Proponents of reform make a substantial case against voluntary discounts on time sold to candidates by broadcasters. Rate reductions vary, even among stations in the same market. Only a small percentage of all stations offers reductions. Voluntary services may be given (and received) as favors by broadcasters to public officials, thereby replacing the obligation that present large contributions impose on candidates. A regulated industry should not be permitted to grant favors to government officials who are in part responsible for regulating them. "End rate" discounts that grant short-term political advertisers the same advantageous rates extended to volume advertisers produce varying savings ranging from substantial to very little. Legislation specifying discounts in such vague terms could lead to abuse. Broadcasters could discontinue or reduce their rates at any time by altering the discounts granted to volume advertisers. Thus rate reductions should be required for all candidates and the percentage of the discount should be specified. Stations should not be permitted to grant discounts in excess of the amount specified. To allow this would encourage a regulated industry to grant favors to candidates. The specified reduction should be no less than 25 percent.

Required sale of time. Congress should impose a reasonable obligation on broadcasters to sell time to candidates. The choice is now left up to broadcasters, and some refuse. The importance of elections justifies removing the sale of time from their whim. Requiring discounts, moreover, increases a station's incentive to refuse to sell time. Discounts will accomplish nothing unless candidates can buy time.[1]

Modification of Section 315. The equal time clause in Section 315 of the Communications Act should be permanently suspended for presidential and vice presidential candidates. The impressive growth of free time provided in recent years on programs that are presently exempt from this requirement justifies liberalizing it further.

The suspension should follow the suggestions of the Federal Communications Commission. Their proposal stipulates that equal time requirements should apply at the presidential level only to significant candidates, which it defines broadly enough to include major third party candidates. By removing the requirement for stations to treat minor and significant candidates equally, the FCC plan removes the chief barrier to provision of free time to presidential candidates. Broadcasters who support suspension of all equal time requirements feel that they can be trusted to treat significant candidates fairly without being required by law to do so. But media advisers to recent Republican and Democratic presidential candidates dispute this claim. They insist that they need the protection of Section 315 (which also requires equal treatment in the selling of time). The FCC plan would provide protection for major candidates as well as relieving stations of the obligation to provide time to minor candidates.[2]

Suspending or modifying Section 315 for candidates below the presidency would at this time generate few benefits. FCC figures show that the number of contenders in senatorial and gubernatorial contests makes no difference in the incidence of free time offered by broadcasters. And Section 315 affords protection to candidates

---

1. Since the 1971 bill stipulates that broadcasters must grant "reasonable" requests for time, this guideline should be fulfilled.

2. For details of the FCC plan, see *The Campaign Broadcast Reform Act of 1969*, Hearing before the Senate Committee on Commerce, 91 Cong. 2 sess. (1969), pp. 74–76.

for lesser offices that they want to keep. It encourages fair treatment and provides a remedy for unfair treatment. Many stations also oppose suspending Section 315, preferring its clearly defined obligations to the more vague "fairness doctrine" that would govern in its absence. For all of these reasons, the disadvantages of suspending Section 315 below the presidency outweigh the advantages of doing so.

Subsidies for television time. The federal government should provide candidates for public office a direct subsidy for the explicit purpose of buying television time. The candidates would negotiate the time purchases with stations or networks, who would bill the national treasury. Candidates should not be required to use their allotted time, and any unused funds designated for television time would remain in the national treasury. Subsidized time should be provided first for presidential candidates. If the subsidy at the presidential level proves desirable, the benefit could be extended to other candidates at a later date, beginning with those in major statewide contests (for U.S. senator and state governor).

This plan could provide major presidential candidates perhaps six thirty-minute program periods and sixty one-minute spot periods. Time for other candidates could be apportioned according to the formula presented in the Twentieth Century Fund's Voters' Time proposal, which divides candidates into three categories. Major party candidates (Category I), representing parties that placed first or second in the preceding election, receive the most time. Third party candidates (Category II), representing parties that received at least one-eighth of the vote in the previous election, receive one-third as much time as candidates in Category I. Candidates representing parties that received less than one-eighth of the vote in the previous election or that were not on the ballot (Category III) receive one-sixth as much time as Category I candidates. All candidates, in order to be eligible for time, must be on the ballots in three-quarters of the states, provided that these states hold a majority of votes in the electoral college.[3]

3. *Voters' Time* (New York: Twentieth Century Fund, 1969).

Subsidized television time can relieve those problems of political broadcasting that modification of Section 315 fails to solve. Changing 315 improves television's ability to provide journalistic coverage of political campaigns. But the candidate has little control over the format of such coverage; he may even find the format (debates, for instance) so distasteful that he refuses to take advantage of free time offers. He needs a means of access to voters in a format he can control. The alternative of buying time that would be paid for by government subsidy gives him that option. It is true that candidate-controlled formats may lead to deceptive presentations, but the problem of providing candidates easier access must be solved on terms that will be acceptable to candidates.

It is possible to make the case that the government should not authorize stations to use the "public airwaves" free of charge and then pay them to broadcast political programs. This looks like a double handout. Requiring free time, however, poses serious problems. It arouses intense opposition among broadcasters, whose considerable influence in the political system almost assures its defeat. Stations require personnel and equipment as well as the "public airwaves" to operate. These cost money and justify some economic return. Publicly subsidized time consequently offers advantages over mandatory free time.

Educational television. Educational television's contribution to past national campaign coverage rates low marks, which leaves room for much future improvement. Public television is better equipped to provide creative programing relevant to national elections under the new government-financed Corporation for Public Broadcasting. The Educational Broadcasting Corporation, formed by the educational stations, has expanded their programing capacity. And a permanent network has linked education stations together since 1970. Public television can use these new instruments to provide alternatives to commercial standards for candidate-voter access. The temptation to increase presidential coverage by plugging the new network into pool coverage of debates or candidate news conferences will be great. But public television should provide programing that is genuinely informative and interesting enough to attract a sizable audience. Its offerings could be more educational than either the present paid programing of candidates or the debates that networks prefer as free time offerings to presidential candidates.

The federal government should provide funds to the Corporation for Public Broadcasting for the explicit purpose of developing independent, high-quality coverage of the 1972 presidential campaign that provides an alternative to present commercial network coverage. The minimum amount of this subsidy should be $1 million. If educational television rises to this challenge (with or without the subsidy), the need to promote greater candidate access through commercial television channels will be considerably reduced.

MAILING SERVICES

The mailing frank that is available to incumbent congressmen during campaigns should be extended to their challengers. Officials cannot now use free mailing privileges for overt political communications, but the definition of "political" is usually construed narrowly. The frank would permit challengers to convey information about their activities and positions on public questions to voters at a fraction of the present cost. Since extending the frank would help only congressional candidates, Congress should extend to other candidates and to party organizations the low postal rates provided to nonprofit charitable organizations. This would assist national parties in direct-mail money solicitation campaigns. It would aid both candidates and party organizations in distributing information to voters.

VOTING REGISTRATION

Through the years, governments have gradually assumed many of the expenses borne by political parties. At one time, parties assumed the cost of ballots and conducting elections, particularly in primaries. Today most states provide state-supported registrars to register qualified voters. For the most part, however, they leave the initiative for registration to the individual. States rarely seek out voters by canvassing precincts and maintaining at state initiative an up-to-date list of all qualified voters.

It is difficult in many states to register at all—some have used this means to discourage voting. Yet before the citizen can vote, he must register. Some studies show that restrictive registration laws explain much of the variation in voter turnout among the states.[4] Parties and candidates in many areas go to phenomenal effort and expense to get their supporters registered. This should be a public effort. The government should provide, at its expense and initiative, an up-to-date voting list of all qualified voters prior to each election. If states desire to undertake this task, the federal government should provide them funds to do it. Otherwise, the federal government should conduct universal registration for federal elections. This could save many candidates and parties vast sums of money.

NATIONAL ELECTION HOLIDAY

A national election holiday (preferably in the middle of the week) is sometimes proposed to generate greater voter turnout. An election holiday might also reduce campaign expenses. Parties and candidates wage "get out the vote" efforts on election day. They create car pools, establish baby sitting services, and canvass the voters they believe to be favorable to them. A holiday would decrease the need for car pools and baby sitting services. Volunteers from among those who would otherwise be working could replace the workers often paid to marshal these election day activities.

Incentives for Private Giving

Reform plans that shift the burden of financing campaigns away from private citizens remove from individuals one means of participating in the electoral process. Contributing can spur voters'

4. See especially Stanley Kelley, Jr., Richard E. Ayres, and William G. Bowen, "Registration and Voting: Putting First Things First," *American Political Science Review*, Vol. 61 (June 1967), pp. 359–79.

interest in a campaign. It can also provide a sanction over office-holders and candidates. This sanction would be even more desirable, of course, if it were exercised by a wider and more evenly distributed group of voters.

Cash benefits plans usually envision more comprehensive reforms, and therefore greater displacement of voter giving, than do service proposals. Even service plans covering several items fail to provide for several crucial expenses that must be financed from private sources. Service plans may therefore loosen the candidate-contributor bond, but they do not break it. The strength of this bond, however, is not at issue, but rather the relative advantages of present as compared with proposed financing methods. The benefits of the donor-candidate bond accrue to only a few—those who give large amounts. Many of the advantages of change, even if only partially realized, would serve a broad spectrum of the electorate. More people, for example, would benefit from more effective use of television for campaign education than would be disadvantaged by less reliance of candidates on private contributors.

If weakening the contributor-candidate bond really worries opponents of change, then their chief concern should be to create the broadest possible base of private contributors. That could be done by establishing programs that would assist candidates to develop a large corps of relatively modest donors, thereby reducing their need to rely on large contributors. This would alleviate some of the more insidious results of private financing. Plans designed to encourage giving by large groups of small contributors could employ a combination of tax incentives and matching grants.

Tax incentives. Tax incentives could take the form of tax credits or deductions. Credits would permit a donor to reduce his income tax obligation by an amount equal to a certain percentage of his contribution to political organizations or candidates. A deduction would allow a taxpayer who itemizes his expenses on his tax return to deduct contributions to political organizations, thus reducing the income upon which he must pay tax.

The combination credit-deduction provided by the 1971 Revenue Act is an excellent method for resolving the impasse between those who have favored one over the other. Although deductions provide more incentive to persons in high tax brackets than to those in low brackets, the credit provision permits all taxpayers to participate, even those who do not itemize their deductions. The Internal Revenue Service will undoubtedly require some documentation of tax savings under these provisions. Congress should closely monitor the performance of the agency in its protection of the confidentiality of taxpayers' reports.

Matching grants. Matching grants could also encourage development of a large base of small contributors. The federal treasury would match the contribution of each donor up to a certain maximum (say, $5, $10, or perhaps $25) dollar for dollar, or at some lower rate. Such a proposal provides parties and candidates an incentive to energetically raise funds from small contributors. The matching grants offset part of the cost of raising the money. They also make it more tempting to go after the small contributor than is now the case.

Restrictions on spending this money should be minimal. The point of incentives is to generate widespread participation through giving, not to encourage or discourage expenditures. The money should, of course, be spent directly for campaign purposes and should be subject to audit by certified public accountants.

Matching grants could be made first at the national level to committees contesting the presidency. If the experiment is successful, it could be extended to other offices and levels that might be difficult to police initially.

The grant plan is plagued by some of the shortcomings of the tax checkoff plans that would permit taxpayers to earmark $1 of their taxes to be used in national presidential campaigns. In both plans, tax money supports parties not supported by all taxpayers. Both face the risk that national parties or candidates will use the money to entrench factions in office. But matching grants have some advantages over tax checkoffs. The proposal suggested here would permit citizens to allocate the money, with the government matching that allocation. It would not remove control of party financing from the citizenry by automatic appropriations—a party would have to raise money from individuals before it was entitled to receive funds from the Treasury.

Avoiding Pitfalls

LIMITATIONS ON EXPENDITURES

This study has not emphasized limiting expenditures as a means of reforming campaign finance. The guidelines suggested here are based on the assumption that the cost of reaching voters is high. The way that candidates must raise the money to pay for modern campaigning creates more problems than does the high cost itself. The best way to reform therefore lies in finding the most neutral means of infusing the present system with money rather than trying to force down the cost of campaigning. Those who support limitations on campaign expenditures believe limitations will prevent further escalation of costs. They argue that limitations must accompany any plan that provides free or reduced cost services to candidates. They also contend that without ceilings, candidates will use the money saved by service plans to buy more of the same for other items.

Past limitation laws were ineffective. They frequently posed unrealistically low ceilings (no more than $5,000 for a House seat, $25,000 for a Senate seat, and $3 million for the presidency, for example).[5] They also provided loopholes that allowed a candidate to report only expenditures of which he had knowledge or permitted an office seeker to create multiple committees, each of which could spend up to the ceiling.

Future limitations should realistically reflect the cost of running for office in the particular election district in which a candidate is waging his campaign. Expenditure reports required by present law

5. The 1971 reform law effectively changed these ceilings.

provide no useful guide to practical limits. Congressional committees possess both the resources and the access to candidates and officials to compile accurate costs if they will take the time to do so. Realistic limits stand a much better chance of being honored than those contrived from "what it ought to cost" or set artificially low.

Future limitations should incorporate flexibility rather than specify fixed amounts for given offices. Campaigning for a U.S. Senate seat costs more in New York or California than in Nevada or Utah. For this reason the best formula would permit *x* cents per voting age person in the given election district. This formula would require frequent Census Bureau calculations to determine the voting age population. Limits based on voting age population have many advantages over those based on actual voting turnout in a given year for a given office. The number voting varies from year to year and from election to election, and is highest in presidential years. More people vote for highly visible offices (presidents and governors) than for less visible ones (House members and state legislators), even in the same election. Between 15 and 20 percent fewer persons vote in off-year elections than in presidential-year elections. No expenditure limit on a candidate for office in 1972 (a presidential year when competition for attention is intense) should be based on the 1970 vote (when turnout was light). Limitations based on voting age population would remain relatively constant from election to election.

Voting participation varies greatly among the states, some having much lower rates of citizen participation than others. Stimulating voters' interest (to activate participation) is a primary purpose of campaigns. Maximum spending formulas based on voting turnout could permanently freeze the discrepancy in participation by limiting the ability of candidates in low-participation states to stimulate voters' interest.

Limitations incorporated in the 1971 broadcasting legislation recognized the merit of basing calculations on voting age population rather than voting turnout. Future legislation should continue to recognize the superiority of this formula, if limitations are to be enacted.

Formulas establishing maximum expenditures should fluctuate with price changes for campaign services. A formula of, say, 20 cents for each voting age individual in a district though adequate for 1972 may not purchase the same services in a later election. Costs may grow faster than the voting age population. For this reason, legislation establishing new limits should authorize construction of an election price index that would measure biennial changes in prices of items commonly used in campaigning. As the new index increased (or decreased), the amount permitted for each voting age person could be adjusted accordingly. This would allow the maximum spending limit to vary in accordance with changes in prices for campaign services. It should keep limitations realistic.

Although the 1970 legislation (vetoed by the President) failed to allow limitations to fluctuate with price changes, the 1971 legislation permitted limitations to respond to increases in the consumer price index. An election price index, however, is a superior instrument for determining changes in campaign expenditure limitations (Figure 5 shows that the cost of some campaign items is rising more rapidly than the consumer price index, for example). It is imperative that an agency (such as the Census Bureau) removed from direct congressional control (unlike the comptroller general or the secretary of the Senate) be responsible for constructing and computing the index. The procedures for constructing the index should be a matter of public record so that independent sources could verify that the changes in the limitation were in response to cost fluctuations rather than to political pressure.

ASSISTANCE TO WHICH CANDIDATES?

Disagreement over which candidates to make eligible for service or cash benefits is an especially divisive issue. Advocates of finance plans that include office seekers below the presidency argue that visible and glamorous presidential candidates can more easily attract adequate financing than candidates for lesser offices. Intense and widespread public scrutiny, moreover, prevents flagrant abuses of candidate-contributor obligations at the presidential level. Their argument that massive change in financing should focus first on lesser offices is impressive.

There is, however, compelling reason to begin at the level of the presidency. The visibility of the office and its high campaign cost dramatize finance problems most effectively. The small number of contenders for the presidency eases the administrative problems of implementing reform. For this reason plans posing particularly difficult organizational problems (such as suspending Section 315 or the matching grant program) should first apply only to presidential candidates. Then as experience warrants they can be extended to other candidates. A next logical expansion for matching grants, for example, would be U.S. senators and representatives. Other plans might be extended to statewide races.

Even though change were limited initially to presidential candidates, other candidates would feel its effects. Campaign finance at various office levels is interrelated. Plans that reduce presidential expenditures, for example, could free money that donors could then funnel to other campaigns. Many suggested plans directly affect all candidates: broadcast rate discounts, tax incentives, government supported registration, and the national voting holiday should provide benefits across the board.

DANGERS OF "DUAL TRACK" FINANCING

Over the long run, American public policy must avoid a "dual track" campaign finance system that provides substantial financial relief for those contesting federal office while providing little or none to candidates for state and local offices. The visibility and growing role of national government obscures the importance of state and local governments, where many decisions affecting the everyday lives and work of Americans are made.

Dual track financing could encourage men without wealth to campaign for federal office, leaving state office as an exclusive preserve of wealthy candidates or contributors. This could worsen the insidious effects of private financing on elections and public policy below the federal level, particularly since many state and local officeholders are under less intense public scrutiny than national officials. It could also intensify problems of recruiting candidates for state and local office.

For these reasons dual track financing should not be permitted. Those reforms that do not immediately provide benefits to state and local, as well as federal, candidates should be extended to all important candidates as soon as short-run experience warrants. In addition, groups active in state government reform should encourage state-directed campaign finance relief. The Council of State Governments and the League of Women Voters have demonstrated interest in the past. They could provide direction for future change.

Summary of Guidelines

Congress should require rate discounts of at least 25 percent on broadcast time for all candidates for public office.

Congress should impose a reasonable obligation on broadcasters to sell time to candidates.

Congress should modify Section 315 (a) of the Communications Act (the equal time clause) for presidential and vice presidential candidates, continuing the protection afforded major candidates while limiting stations' obligations to minor candidates.

Congress should provide presidential candidates a subsidy to purchase fixed amounts of broadcast time.

Congress should provide a subsidy to the Corporation for Public Broadcasting to stimulate the development by educational television of high-quality alternatives to present commercial methods of covering presidential campaigns.

Congress should extend the mailing frank currently available to incumbent U.S. senators and representatives to their challengers during the election campaign. The low postal rates provided to nonprofit charitable organizations should be extended to other candidates and to party organizations.

Congress should provide for an up-to-date voting list of all qualified voters prior to each election. If states desire to undertake this task, federal funds should be provided to them. Otherwise, the federal government should conduct universal registration for federal elections.

Congress should declare a national election holiday, preferably in the middle of the week, for the day on which the general election is held.

Congress should continue the tax incentives included in the Revenue Act of 1971. It should institute a plan for the federal government to match each dollar raised by a political party up to a certain maximum.

Congress should not impose limitations on expenditures. They are difficult to enforce and have often in the past confounded efforts to get full disclosure of actual campaign expenditures. If limitations are adopted, however, they should be practical and flexible, based on voting age population in the constituency covered by the given office, and free to change in response to changes in a price index of campaign costs.

Finance reform should begin first at the presidential level and be extended to other offices later. Reform at the state level should not be neglected.

Prospects for Change

The leading prospect for further change is the tax checkoff provision of the Revenue Act of 1971 that permits taxpayers to direct $1 of their tax money to a major party nominee or a nonpartisan fund. Because there are those who favor blocking its implementation, it is appropriate to pinpoint some of the difficulties, and advantages, of this legislation. The service package solution outlined earlier is preferable to the tax checkoff plan, but if the checkoff is to be implemented, it ought first to be improved.

The tax checkoff plan, it has been charged, would permit the government to use tax moneys to finance candidates whom some taxpayers oppose. But the taxpayer's proprietary right to money he has paid in taxes is not well established in this country. Moreover, the individual taxpayer's choice is a dubious standard by which to judge a given public activity, and it is not applied in other policy areas. A large number of people whose taxes support the social security program would prefer that their money be used for other purposes, and opponents of the Vietnam war deplore the use of their tax dollars for that purpose. Their preferences are no less important than those of taxpayers who oppose support of nominees for public office.

The right of taxpayers to designate where given tax dollars will go—for funding campaigns rather than some other public purpose—raises the possibility that earmarking will become common in financing public programs. Although the checkoff is a serious threat as a precedent, the objection is weakened by the provision that requires an actual appropriation by Congress, rather than automatic diversion of tax money. Indeed, the outcome would be unchanged if the checkoff were eliminated and the appropriation retained.

The checkoff plan also raises the issue of confidentiality. Those who designate their funds for a party nominee will thereby make a public record (small contributions are not now reported at the national level). Once collected by the Internal Revenue Service, such information becomes one more piece of datum about a citizen that can be stored and used for a variety of purposes. One resolution of this issue might be to strictly oversee the work of the Internal Revenue Service, stipulating stringent guidelines for handling the record. An even better solution would be to appropriate money directly from the public treasury, thus precluding collection of one more item of information about a large group of citizens.

The tax checkoff plan also imposes spending limitations—fifteen cents per voting age citizen in a given election year—on those who opt for public financing. One of the many difficulties of enforcing such limitations is in allocating among candidates the common expenditures made on behalf of an entire ticket. Moreover, where do local and state expenditures for broadcasting time, halls in which rallies are held, rental cars, and other single-performance expenses belong? Limitations also may benefit incumbents who do not have to spend as much as their challengers, and they potentially violate first amendment rights since they may prevent a citizen from spending money to advance his preferences.

The tax checkoff plan, like other reform proposals, may inhibit citizens' participation in public processes by reducing their incentive to contribute to candidates. Such participation is not widespread, however, and its rewards accrue disproportionately to those who give large sums of money. Moreover, some 500,000 elective offices unaffected by the tax checkoff will provide opportunities for those who wish to participate.

That a campaign subsidy will markedly depress the rise of new parties is unlikely. An even stronger barrier to new parties is the limitation of expenditures, since unknown parties must spend more than the established to make a good showing. The tax checkoff plan does provide money to nominees of parties that poll at least 5 percent of the vote—funds not previously available for the advancement of new parties.

In fact, perpetuation of the status quo through a government campaign subsidy is no more feared than proliferation of candidacies. Although proliferation is a possibility under any plan, it is a stronger one with money than with service plans. The requirement of posting at least 5 percent of the votes in order to accrue benefits may be high enough at least to damp proliferation.

Because the tax checkoff plan covers only postconvention expenses, the preconvention campaign may become the focus of fatcats' money and influence. One possible solution to this problem would be to extend the benefits of the plan to preconvention campaigns, particularly those involving presidential primary elections. Although criteria of eligibility would be difficult to establish, a commission might be charged with identifying presidential candidates (much as is done in states that require all serious candidates to appear on the presidential primary ballot), or the benefits might be vested in all who are favored by, say, 5 percent in preconvention public opinion polls. The checkoff plan should not be discarded simply because the preconvention campaign is a problem. One solution is to let experience accumulate before dealing with the problem; an alternative is to act now to include primaries under the provisions of the plan.

The tax checkoff plan also has some advantages. At the expense of permitting taxpayers to earmark tax money, it does retain some direct citizen control over the amount of money candidates will receive. And it embodies the general advantages that accrue to cash benefit plans, providing more comprehensive relief, establishing a larger gross amount of assistance, and promoting greater flexibility in candidates' use of resources than do service plans. No other proposal designed to provide substantial resources for campaigning has twice achieved the status of law during the last five years.

The problems associated with the tax checkoff measure, while common to many reform plans, tend to be exacerbated in those that provide cash benefits. That is why the guidelines discussed earlier in this chapter concentrate on a service package as the preferable method of reform. If political exigencies admit only the checkoff plan, the most difficult problems associated with it should be remedied.

Despite the impediments to reform in campaign financing and the preference of many influential participants in the policy arena for the certainties of present practices, there are signs of change. The public may be moving from its lethargy as the electoral and policy consequences of present financing methods become more widely recognized. Public awareness may continue to stimulate interest among officials, who will reshuffle their priorities and begin to pursue change. Incumbents may ease their resistance to reform as they increasingly find their own campaign costs soaring. Passage by both houses of Congress of campaign reforms in 1970 and 1971 marks the first concrete signs of change. As barriers continue to fall, reformers can concentrate on broadening the coverage of the country's laws to move closer to achieving democratic elections.

Appendix

BROADCAST QUESTIONNAIRE

IN FEBRUARY 1970 a broadcast questionnaire was sent to the general managers of 150 television stations chosen by a random number table from a list of all but fifteen television stations licensed to operate in the United States (as found in the 1969 *Broadcasting Yearbook*). The fifteen excluded were network-owned stations; an executive of each of these networks was personally interviewed.

The initial individually typed and signed letter (Exhibit A) and accompanying questionnaire (Exhibit B) were followed by a brief postcard reminder to nonrespondents approximately three weeks later. Two weeks after that a lithographed letter and a new questionnaire were sent to the remaining nonrespondents. Responses were received from 91 managers, 60.7 percent of the group solicited.

EXHIBIT A

February 11, 1970

Dear Mr. _____:

The Brookings Institution is currently studying several proposals which their proponents claim would drive down political campaign costs by making television less costly to political advertisers.

Any such study would be unfair and incomplete if it ignored the impact of these plans on local stations. No one is better qualified to speak from the practical perspective of local broadcasters than persons like yourself. That is why we ask the benefit of your experience by requesting that you complete the enclosed questionnaire.

The questionnaire is designed for rapid completion. All replies will be confidential.

With kindest regards,

Cordially,

Del Dunn

BROOKINGS BROADCAST QUESTIONNAIRE

The questions require little writing. Additional comments will be most welcome.

Your answers will be held in strict confidence and will never be identified either with you personally or with your station. They will be grouped together with the responses from all other stations, counted, and statistically analyzed in much the same way that individual responses are grouped and analyzed in national opinion polls.

The number at the top of this page identifies your station to us. When we receive your response it will inform us that we will not have to send follow-up reminders and permit us to acknowledge its receipt. We will then separate the number from the questionnaire and never associate it with your station.

You were chosen by a random selection process which permits a fair and accurate representation of all members of a group (in this instance all commercial television stations in the United States) by getting the responses of only part of the group—in this instance 150 stations of which you are one. This is the exact principle which such rating services as Nielsen use to determine program audience ratings.

The Brookings Institution is a private, nonpartisan research institution which is noted for its scholarly, impartial, and objective studies about government policy questions. If you have further questions about Brookings, they may be answered by referring to the enclosed brochure.

Your willingness to complete this questionnaire will be most appreciated.

1. Primary Network affiliation

   ☐ ABC   ☐ CBS   ☐ NBC   ☐ None

   ☐ Other (please specify) _____

2. Type of station

   ☐ UHF   ☐ VHF

3. Estimated market size _____

4. Some advocate changing Section 315 of the Communications Act in order to free stations to give more time to major candidates, if the station desires to do so. What is your position on this matter?

   ☐ Leave as is

☐ Change to permit giving major candidates time without obligating station to provide time for minor candidates

☐ No opinion

☐ Other (please specify) _____

_____

5. (If you favor leaving Section 315 of the Communications Act as it is, please answer this question. Others skip to question 6.)
Why do you favor leaving Section 315 of the Communications Act as it is? (Check as many as applicable.)

☐ It provides clear guidelines about the station's responsibility and obligations in political broadcasting.

☐ The station would be more vulnerable to attack during campaigns if 315 were not on the law books.

☐ We would lose control of our ability to schedule candidates without Section 315.

☐ No opinion

☐ Other (please specify) _____

_____

6. Regardless of your opinion about suspending 315, *if* it were suspended, what candidates should such a suspension apply to?

☐ President and Vice President only

☐ All elected federal officials

☐ All elected federal officials and the state governor

☐ All elected officials

☐ No opinion

☐ Other (please specify) _____

_____

7. If Section 315 were changed in order that stations would not have to give time to fringe candidates, what would be the likely reaction of your station?
(Check as many as applicable.)

☐ We would give more time to presidential candidates.

☐ We would give additional time to candidates for statewide and federal office.

☐ We would give more time to local contests with wide interest.

☐ It is not likely that we would give more time for any candidates.

☐ No opinion

☐ Other (please specify) _____

8. Some officials fear that if stations were not restricted by Section 315 they would provide one-sided presentations as some contend that newspapers now do. Is this concern justified?

☐ Yes   ☐ No   ☐ No opinion

☐ Other (please specify) _____

9. Candidates for what offices qualify to purchase program-length time (longer than five minutes) on your station?

10. Do political candidates generally prefer program length or "spot" time for political advertising?

☐ Program length   ☐ Spot

☐ Other (please specify) _____

11. Do you always have spot availabilities for candidates who want them or is the demand greater than the supply of time?

☐ Always have been available

☐ Usually are available, sometimes requires negotiation with candidates

☐ Demand for time is often greater than supply

☐ Other (please specify) _____

12. Do you charge the local or national rate for political advertisements?

☐ The local rate for all candidates

☐ The national rate for all candidates

☐ The local rate for local candidates and the national rate for statewide candidates

☐ Other (please specify) _____

---

13. In the last national election year (1968) what percentage of your station's gross revenues was derived from political advertising?

☐ Less than 1 percent   ☐ 1–5 percent   ☐ 6–10 percent

☐ Greater than 10 percent

Two plans recently presented are designed, according to their advocates, to reduce political campaign costs by requiring television stations to reduce their rates to political candidates. The next few questions pertain to these plans.

14. The Campaign Broadcast Reform Act, currently pending in the U.S. Senate and House of Representatives has the following basic provisions:

    a. For candidates for the House of Representatives the bill provides 60 one-minute prime-time spots at 30 percent of the regular rate and one thirty-minute program at 20 percent of the regular rate. All stations located within the geographic boundaries of the congressional district plus those stations outside the district which serve at least one-third of the population of the district within their A-contour broadcast area would have to divide equally the responsibility of making the time at reduced rates available. The candidate would pay the broadcasting charge at the reduced rates.

    b. For U.S. Senate candidates the bill provides 120 one-minute spots and one thirty-minute program at the same rate reductions specified above. All stations within the state plus those outside the state with at least one-fifth of their A-contour audience within the state would divide equally the responsibility of making the time at reduced rates available.

What is your opinion of this proposal?

☐ I favor it.   ☐ I oppose it.

☐ I favor it with modifications.   ☐ No opinion

☐ Other (please specify) _____

If you have no opinion or do not oppose the legislation, please skip to question 16.

15. Why do you oppose this legislation? (Check as many as applicable.)

☐ It discriminates against one industry.

☐ I don't want to see rate regulation.

☐ Providing political candidates with reduced rates for political advertising would set a precedent which might be applied to other areas in the future.

☐ Other (please specify) _____

16. Another proposal would provide a total of up to six prime-time thirty-minute programs for major party candidates (less for third party candidates) for each presidential and vice presidential candidate. Each program would be broadcast simultaneously over every broadcast and cable television facility. The federal government would pay for the time at a rate no greater than 50 percent of the commercial rate for the time.

What do you think of this proposal?

☐ I favor it.   ☐ I oppose it.   ☐ No opinion

☐ Other (please specify) _____

17. If you oppose it: Would you state briefly why you oppose it?

_____

_____

_____

INDEX

Adamany, David, 125
Alexander, Herbert E., 13n, 31n, 32n, 61n, 81n, 130n; on debate format, 100; on fund raising, 109; on national committees, 76–77; on television costs, 42
American Association of Political Consultants, 64
American Broadcasting Companies, 76
American Independent party (AIP), 63, 88, 99
Anderson, John, 51n, 52, 57
Ayres, Richard E., 147n

Berelson, Bernard, 3n, 60n
Bernstein, Marver, 70n
Bird, Agnes, 3n, 126n
Blumler, Jay G., 6n
Bowen, William G., 147n
Broadcasters: debate format, 84–85, 95–100; equal time rule, 82–83, 133–37, 143; fairness doctrine, 118, 136, 144; format regulation, 105, 126–29, 145; free time attitude, 82–95, 105–6, 120; minor party attitude, 82, 86, 88, 94, 102; profits, 65–66, 114, 120, 129–31; rate discount attitude, 53, 71, 120, 129–38, 141–42; reform attitude, 65–69, 73, 120–21; regulation rationale, 117–20; service package proposal, 141–47; spending limits proposal, 48–50, 59, 113, 139; subsidy proposal, 144–45, 154; voluntary service plans, 120, 138. *See also* Radio; Television
Buchanan, William, 3n, 126n
Bullitt, Stimson, 106, 129, 130n
Burch, Dean, 71

Campbell, Angus, 3n, 4n, 60n
Canadian Broadcasting Corporation, 98
Candidate: *1970* reform bill, 46–49; broadcast format, 99–100, 105, 145;

contributor commitment, 14–16, 21–25; governor, 48, 91, 93, 122, 144; incumbent v. challenger, 4, 6–8, 24, 50, 58–59, 75–76, 100, 157–58; media image, 4–5; minor party, 47, 55–56, 154; political consultant use, 29–30; and poll-taking, 29–30; presidential, 40–41, 46–49, 54–56, 82–88, 93–94, 99–100, 114–16, 122–25, 137–38, 143–44, 152–53; representative, U.S., 48, 55, 76–77, 122, 124, 153; senator, U.S., 48, 55, 76–77, 91, 93, 122, 124, 144, 153; state and local, 94–95, 153–55; wealthy v. nonwealthy, 11–14. *See also* Public official
CED. *See* Committee for Economic Development
Challenger. *See* Candidate
Columbia Broadcasting System, 83–84
Committee for Economic Development (CED), 53, 57, 72
Communications Act, 46–48, 51, 71, 82–95. *See also* Section 315(a), Communications Act
Congressman. *See* Representative, U.S.; Senator, U.S.
Conservative Party of New York State, 102
Contributor: *1971* reform proposal, 50–51; current law, 51, 57; Democratic party, 61; implicit commitments, 21–25; interests of, 16–18; large, 11–14, 59, 82, 109–10, 123; motivations, 16–18; participation factor, 74, 79–81, 121, 147–48, 157; power of, 19–25, 78, 81–82; public norms, 14–16; reform attitude, 59; reform proposals, 50–51, 57, 147–50; Republican party, 59–61; small, 60–61, 109–10; tax credit-deduction proposals, 54, 61, 77,

165